The Atlantic Idea and Its European Rivals

Published volumes in the series
"The Atlantic Policy Studies"

HENRY A. KISSINGER
The Troubled Partnership:
A Re-appraisal of the Atlantic Alliance

ZBIGNIEW BRZEZINSKI
Alternative to Partition: For a
Broader Conception of America's Role in Europe

JOHN O. COPPOCK
Atlantic Agricultural Unity:
Is It Possible?

HAROLD VAN B. CLEVELAND
The Atlantic Idea and Its
European Rivals

The Atlantic Idea
and
Its European Rivals

HAROLD VAN B. CLEVELAND

A Volume in the series
"The Atlantic Policy Studies"

Published for the Council on Foreign Relations by

McGRAW-HILL BOOK COMPANY
New York   Toronto   London   Sydney

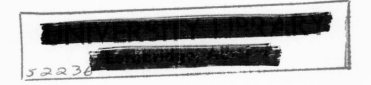

THE ATLANTIC IDEA AND ITS EUROPEAN RIVALS

Library of Congress Catalog Card Number: 66-24473
First Edition
11373

TO JOAN

who wrote this book with me

Foreword

Because of the central role the author of this volume has played in the series of publications by the Council on Foreign Relations known as the Atlantic Policy Studies, this foreword should begin with a word of description on this project. This program of studies was made possible by a substantial grant by the Ford Foundation in mid-1962, the general purpose of which was to conduct an examination in depth of Atlantic relationships and the factors bearing upon the evolution of the groupings of the principal North American and European states. The formulation and execution of the studies was left to the Council.

To plan and carry out this unusual undertaking, the Council set up a special and semi-autonomous series of groups. A small committee was charged with the original formulation and staffing of the project which was later enlarged into the Steering Committee, which has had over-all responsibility for the guidance and supervision of the program. The normal Council process was, however, preserved, in that the authors of each of the books which was commissioned, worked in collaboration with a group of experts drawn from government and the academic world and from business and the professions, according to the Council pattern.

Since the full length books which have been or will be published under this program number ten, this study group technique involved the organization of an extensive consultative apparatus. The Steering Committee, which brought together a number of men of experience and sophistication in the field, in addition to serving as the authorizing body for the entire series, constituted itself a study group for studies of a political nature, including the present volume and two prospective volumes—a study by Miriam Camps of the recent evolution and future prospects of the European Economic Community and an adaptation of a series of lectures before the Council by Stanley Hoffmann dealing with the constraints upon foreign policy inherent in the American governmental system. The members of the Steering Committee are: Hamilton F. Armstrong, Gabriel Hauge, Henry A. Kissinger, Klaus Knorr, Ben T. Moore, Alfred C. Neal, James A. Perkins, Eugene V. Rostow, Arnold Wolfers and David MacEachron, Secretary, John J. McCloy, Grayson Kirk, Frank Altschul and George S. Franklin, Jr. are *ex officio* members. It has been my privilege to serve as Chairman of the Steering Committee.

The separate group which dealt with two volumes devoted to the "external environment" of the Atlantic Community, Zbigniew Brzezinski's "Alternative to Partition," published in the spring of 1965, and a volume by Theodore Geiger, planned for publication early in 1967, was chaired by Eugene V. Rostow. Klaus Knorr was chairman of the group which considered Henry A. Kissinger's volume *The Troubled Partnership: Re-Appraisal of the Atlantic Alliance* published in 1965. Alfred C. Neal was chairman of the group on Atlantic trade and economic arrangements. Several specific works in this field were also assisted by *ad hoc* groups for the volumes in question. A two-volume work on Atlantic trade and economic arrangements by Bela Balassa scheduled for publication early in 1967 was considered by a study group headed by William F. Butler. Richard N. Cooper, whose study will deal with Atlantic monetary arrangements, was assisted by a study group headed by Gardner Patterson. Isaiah Frank is chairman of the study group which has worked with John A. Pincus on a volume dealing with the Atlantic Community and the underdeveloped countries, scheduled for publication late in 1966. And finally, a study group chaired by D. Gale Johnson assisted John O. Coppock in his book published early in 1966 entitled *Atlantic Agricultural Unity: Is It Possible?*

Thus the Council tenet that the work of an author of a Council publication, while remaining the full responsibility of the author, is seasoned and informed by discussions among knowledgeable colleagues of varied but relevant experience has been consistently applied in the development of these studies. The chairmen and members of these advisory study groups deserve the warm thanks of the Council for the commitment of their time, thought and critical faculties to this multi-faceted project.

"Van" Cleveland's place in the Atlantic Policy Studies deserves a word of special comment. From the inception of the project he has served as Director of the Studies. Mr. Cleveland was selected by the officers of the Council and the Steering Committee to direct the project not only by reason of his natural aptitudes and executive capabilities, but because of his extensive experience both within and outside government during the early postwar period, as well as his continuing interest in and exposure to the field of study. Particularly with reference to United States policy toward European unification, Mr. Cleveland had been one of the small circle of government officials whose thinking and writing had had much to do with the shaping of United States policy of the early fifties. Mr. Cleveland has had a major part in the planning of the Atlantic Policy Studies and the continuing supervision necessary to carry them into effect, including collaboration with the authors in the various stages of their work, from outlining their presentation to editorial assistance in preparing for publication.

It had been planned from the beginning that, in addition to his executive functions, Mr. Cleveland would write a concluding volume which, hopefully, would reflect the conclusions from the various studies. This volume is the fruition of that plan. Because of time considerations which were beyond the control of the Council and Mr. Cleveland, his volume appears chronologically somewhat before the median publication point and not as the final volume in the program. Notwithstanding this fact, Mr. Cleveland's work with the authors, both those who have already published and those who have not, over a period of two and a half years, has, I believe, stimulated his thinking and contributed to the formulation of his views expressed in this volume.

As Mr. Cleveland states in the introductory chapter, his study "is about the dynamics of Atlantic politics in the 1960's." His treatment of this very broad subject is analytical and not prescriptive. He seeks to identify the forces which bear upon the present structure of relationships in the European and Atlantic Communities, analyzing the forces that hold the Atlantic states together and the forces that tend to divide them. Although the book is written with the perspective of an American critic and commentator, it stops short of attempting to outline policy for the United States.

Mr. Cleveland's systematic identification of the centripetal and centrifugal forces is set against a fresh and useful statement of the nature of international politics in the 1960's, which forms the conceptual background for his analysis. International politics no longer deals with classic territorial or ethnic quarrels, nor with parochial strategic advantage, nor with colonial rivalries. The subject matter of international political dialogue now is the working of and the control over the system of economic and political agencies and international institutions that have been created during the past two decades and characterize international relations of the mid-1960's. International conflicts now largely take place within the general framework of these institutions and, in most important respects, turn upon the question of who defines the common interest and who determines the common policy within this framework. As Mr. Cleveland points out, this is a process that is much more akin to domestic political manoeuvering than to the classic subject matter of international politics.

As the title of the volume indicates, Mr. Cleveland has chosen to put his analysis in terms of the juxtaposition and the conflict of, and the competition between, the "European idea" and the "Atlantic idea." He defines "idea" not as an abstraction but as a "tendency or purpose which seeks to realize or maintain itself in actuality," that is, as an organizing concept. This contrapuntal theme appears and reappears throughout the opening chapters, which are organized functionally and which deal with security and the control of nuclear power, with the monetary problem and with the questions lurking in the area of international trade. Mr. Cleveland points out an interesting parallel between the security and monetary fields. In each case the facts of contemporary life, as to the distribution of nuclear and economic power, force upon the Atlantic Community greater interdependence, carrying with it the dominant position of the United States. In each case this is accompanied by increasing debate and sharpening conflict as to the control of the existing international mechanisms and as to the control of and the political purposes for which any substitute mechanisms might be devised. Strictures of time prevented Mr. Cleveland from carrying his analysis through the other fields in which the competition between the European and Atlantic ideas presumably exists, particularly the impact upon each of the underdeveloped world and its problems. Also, the emerging problem of agriculture in the European and Atlantic context, which is the subject of Mr. Coppock's illuminating study published this spring, is developed less fully than might have been the case had this study been published a year from now.

Mr. Cleveland's concluding analysis of the "European idea" leaves one with the feeling that this concept has seen better days. The "classical" European doctrine which developed in the early postwar years rested on the assumption that Europe could never achieve military security, political stability or economic growth without supranational European economic and political institutions. This concept, fathered by Jean Monnet and adopted by most prominent Americans in positions of responsibility at the time, received wide acceptance and gave rise to expectations that have proved overly optimistic. The force of this concept seems to have been diluted by the fact that Europe has in fact found ways to achieve military security, political stability and a high degree of economic growth with only rudimentary supranational economic institutions. This, according to Mr. Cleveland, has removed the urgency and dampened the spirit which moved the early "Europeans." Another inhibiting factor has been the recognition that European security depends upon extra-European forces—another way of saying that the European idea is less than adequate for European purposes in the mid-1960's. And a supposed incentive toward European unity,—the desire for equal partnership with the United States—does not appear to have sufficient lift to move Europeans to a major act of political reconstruction. Finally, the impact of French and British policy upon the European idea is examined and for wholly different reasons (the nationalism of the French and the indifference of the British) is found to be negative. All of this leads to the conclusion that the European idea has lost much of the dynamism of a decade ago and does not seem appropriate as the central concept for organizing the Atlantic world.

But if the European idea has lost much of its force as an organizing concept, it is not because of the greater power of the Atlantic idea. In his concluding chapter on the Atlantic idea, Mr. Cleveland finds in it no standard to which Atlantic peoples can be moved to repair or any basis for agreement among their governments, but an existing, cold, inescapable equilibrium of forces. The Atlantic Community (which is a coalition and not a "community" in the true sense) is cohesive only because of American nuclear power which exercises for all of the states of the Atlantic the basic function of national defense. This power exists *de facto* and not by the consent of the defended, and its unilateral exercise by the United States is a factor which divides us from our allies, and also creates malaise and feelings of guilt among Americans. For our values hold "that cooperation and consensus, not conflict, are the norm in international relations and that power without consent is *ipso facto* evil." In the security sphere there is no acceptable alternative to this unwelcome state of facts.

The Atlantic grouping, viewed as an economic community, might well increase its present measure of interdependence by agreement, since the economic systems of the principal Atlantic powers are now similarly organized and are hospitably inclined toward integration. Thus a "partnership" might be approached or achieved in relation to economic matters which is dubious or impossible in respect of security. But here too one should not underestimate the viability or the virulence of the national viewpoint.

Mr. Cleveland suggests that Americans should not be too unhappy with the present state of affairs which has served American interests well for the past decade or so. For despite the tensions with our Atlantic allies, as well as our adversaries, the peace has been preserved, economic growth has exceeded all expectations and in the Atlantic area political stability has been achieved, and within a political framework and climate in which democratic institutions have been permitted to develop, most importantly in Germany. Perhaps our greatest difficulty is self-inflicted, that is, the over-expectation that has existed among Americans, generated by the plans and institutional blueprints and their optimistic projections of the course of both the European and Atlantic ideas. Mr. Cleveland's final admonition is that Americans should become accustomed to the exercise of national power and to the fact that conflict is normal in relations between states. And since the United States alone has the power to assure the continuation of the benefits of the unplanned system which has forced these responsibilities upon it, it should continue to act wisely and in its enlightened self-interest, in concert with its allies where possible and unilaterally where it is not.

This conclusion of Mr. Cleveland's volume is not a call to action stations nor an exhortation to repair to the ancient values of either the European or the Atlantic ideas. It is a careful, dispassionate and measured analysis of the forces which have shaped our present political environment and a rational reminder that we should look to the essentials of this environment and make the best of them. His analysis brings a fresh point of view to a debate which has often become stale and doctrinaire. It should be a provocative and useful tool for those who, by professional interest or by inclination, are students of the problems of Europe and North America.

CHARLES M. SPOFFORD
New York, June 1966

Preface

In 1945, many embers smouldered in the ashes of Europe and thoughtful, responsible, above all hopeful men considered how the destructive embers could be put out and how the warmth and light of the promising ones could be fanned into flame. The policies they formulated in those years were remarkable, and even the most hopeful of men would scarcely have predicted the present condition of Europe. But things have not only improved; they have also changed.

When we started to think about this book, we shared the belief, widely held both in America and in Europe, that the nation state, in this region of the world, was a dying institution. With many others, we expected that it would soon give way to supranationalism, first in Western Europe and then perhaps in the entire Atlantic region. In the course of our exploration we had to question whether the facts bore out this belief. We have concluded that they do not. Although the content and spirit of nationalism in the Atlantic region have profoundly changed, the nation-state system is still with us, and, we think, will remain the dominant pattern of political organization.

We have, therefore, neither presumed that Europe is moving toward supranational unity nor that relations between states are essentially similar to what they were before the War. Both the character of the national actors and the nature of their relationships have changed in ways quite unforeseen when the supranational hopes and visions of the '40s and '50s were first conceived. The result is a kind of international community in the Atlantic region, the nature of which still largely remains to be defined. In this book we have tried in some measure to define it.

Although we must bear alone the responsibility for the conclusions of this book, we are gratefully indebted to many friends and colleagues for their help, encouragement and criticism. We would like to express our special gratitude to Charles M. Spofford, Chairman of the Steering Committee of the Atlantic Policy Studies, for his time, interest and concern. His constant encouragement, his willingness to re-examine inherited formulations and commitments, and his personal consideration made this book possible. The members of the Steering Committee discussed the manuscript chapter by chapter at a series of meetings and contributed many valuable individual comments as well.

George S. Franklin, Jr., Executive Director of the Council on Foreign Relations, William Diebold, Jr., Senior Research Fellow of the Council, Miriam Camps of the Council and the Royal Institute of International Affairs, and David MacEachron, the Council's Associate Executive Director for Program, merit special thanks for their careful and detailed observations on the text. Judd Polk, of the National Industrial Conference Board, read and commented on Chapter 5. David Robison made many thoughtful suggestions on the military chapters. This is also the place to acknowledge his outstanding work and loyal service as rapporteur of the Steering Committee and all other committees and study groups of the Council's Atlantic Policy Studies.

To the Ford Foundation, and especially to John J. Mc-Cloy, Shepherd Stone and Joseph Slater, go our special thanks for making the Atlantic Policy Studies possible and for many lively and useful discussions of Atlantic policy issues.

Janet Rigney, surely the most imaginative librarian there is, reliably filled our requests, however impossible or vague. We are grateful also to Emilio Mesa, who handled so much of the mechanics of the job so skillfully and to Ruth Saks, our secretary at the start of this project, who coped cheerfully with chaos. Ellen Choffin combined the functions of secretary and research and administrative assistant and performed them all with a very high degree of efficiency and intelligence. We could never have gotten along without her.

Finally, we must acknowledge four special debts. To Theodore and Frances Geiger, who read the entire manuscript and lent us their perceptiveness to illuminate dark and murky corners of the argument, and to Gertrude Tilly and Diana Cleveland, who coped with us through it all, and without whose patient and compassionate loyalty this book could not have been written.

This preface and the chapters which follow are written in the first person plural because they were co-authored by my wife, Joan B. Cleveland. The original concept, the principal ideas, and the conclusions are the product of many weeks of discussion and writing together. Few authors, I expect, can truthfully say that writing a book is fun, but the companionship and mutual support which this collaboration afforded were for us the best part.

Harold van B. Cleveland
New York, New York

Contents

Introduction

For twenty years the nations of Western Europe and North America have enjoyed a relationship which is unique and unprecedented. These nations have come to constitute a "community" in a sense of the word which is more than metaphorical.

Because it does not fit traditional categories, the Atlantic Community is not easy to describe. It is a military alliance but it is more than an alliance. Despite two decades of peace in Europe, it still has more cohesion than many a coalition in wartime. Its long duration and institutionalized character are inconsistent with traditional notions of national military autonomy.

The Atlantic Community is an economic community as well as a military alliance. The economies of the Atlantic allies are more integrated with one another and with a few other Western countries and Japan than any other group of independent national economies has ever been. The accomplishment is the more remarkable because, in this day of enlarged public responsibility for economic life, integration presupposes a willingness by governments to qualify their sovereign autonomy in economic matters by cooperation unprecedented in kind and in degree.

Political relations among the Atlantic allies also differ from traditional relations among sovereign states. In the immediate postwar period, the politics of the Atlantic Community were remarkable for their harmony. American leadership in the tasks of European recovery and defense was eagerly sought. Many Europeans were concerned that there would be too little rather than too much of the American presence, too restrained rather than too vigorous an American leadership. Busy with the wreckage of war, deeply disillusioned with nationalism, Europeans were willing to leave the definition of common interests and the making of common policies to Americans. Western Europe felt too insecure militarily, too much in need of American aid, and too dependent on American political support to define its interests as inconsistent in any important degree with American interests. Americans, despite their isolationist past, were not backward about accepting this new and satisfying role, in which idealistic impulse, national interest, and will to power so harmoniously blended. American leadership provided the coordination of effort needed for common tasks too large to be efficiently undertaken by nations acting autonomously.

With recovery in Western Europe and *détente* in the East-West confrontation, this harmonious conjuncture has changed, as it was bound to, and political conflict has again made its appearance among the nations of the West. But Atlantic politics in the 1960s are not international politics as usual, if the measure of what is usual is prewar Europe. Both the content and the spirit have profoundly changed.

Military and economic interdependence has transformed the nature of the political issues which divide the West. Today's issues bear little resemblance to the peripheral territorial and ethnic quarrels, the struggles over minor strategic assets, the colonial and commercial rivalries of the classical European politics. Still less do they resemble the bitter ideological-nationalist struggle of the 1930s between Hitler and the Western democracies.

In the 1960s the principal subject mater of Atlantic politics is the structure, the locus of control, and the policies of the great systems of military and economic cooperation which have grown up since 1945. Not Alsace-Lorraine but the role of the European Commission; not the control of the Dardanelles or the rights of national minorities in Central Europe, but NATO strategy and the control of nuclear weapons; not the choice between totalitarian fascism and democracy but between the dollar and the CRU—such are the functional and technical matters which provide the main stuff of international politics in the Atlantic world today. In its subject matter, Atlantic politics has come to resemble the internal politics of integral political communities. It deals mainly with issues of a kind which in former times were the exclusive province of domestic politics.

The spirit, too, has been transformed. The nationalism of the Western nations has a quite different quality than it used to have. It no longer has its former chauvinistic, xenophobic, or isolationist overtones, still less the aggressive and imperialist animus of nazism and fascism. It is restrained, unideological, and on the whole rather tame. Nationalism it still is. For all their supranational visions, the Western peoples have no higher political commitment than to their national communities. But the tone and spirit of that commitment are no longer incompatible with respect for one another, nor with functional cooperation.

No doubt this transformation owes much to the psychological impact of the war and to the increase in mutual knowledge which has come with improved communications. More fundamentally, it is due to the experience, long continued, of military and economic interdependence, which has reduced the significance of national identity. The nation-states are dwarfed by the immense geographical scope of their economic and security problems. It reflects also the marked convergence since 1945 of political, social, and economic values and institutions, and of economic conditions, among the Western nations—most notably, the rebirth of constitutional democracy in Germany and Italy—a convergence which has been the result of increased contact with and emulation of American society, whose prestige has been enhanced by military and economic success.

It is hardly surprising in the circumstances that the mainstreams of American postwar thought about the Atlantic Community have flowed from the premise that nationalism and the national state are obsolescent. Two expectations have been derived from this premise. One is that harmony and cooperation among the Atlantic nations will increasingly prevail over discord and conflict. The other is that increasing functional cooperation will lead in time to a voluntary merger of national sovereignties into supranational political structures.

For alliance and cooperation (so the argument runs), although necessary, are not enough. The manifest inefficiency of divided management of international money and trade, the manifest inequity of unilateral American control of strategy and nuclear weapons in the Alliance, the manifest need to pool Western resources for security and economic development in the Third World and to allocate the benefits and burdens equitably, must lead sooner or later to a fundamental institutional change in which supranational agencies assume control of the key functions and facilities: military strategy and nuclear weapons; international monetary policy and the creation and distribution of international money; trade policy and trade barriers; development aid. In time it will prove necessary to legitimize the immense power of the functional agencies by a constituent political act, and to subject them to democratic control by the elected representatives of the peoples in supranational parliament assembled.

One school has thought of this evolution from cooperation to supranationalism as taking place among the entire group of Atlantic nations; that is, the members of the Atlantic Alliance (or most of them), plus the European neutrals, perhaps. Another school, and the one which has most directly influenced official policy, stresses the difference between the United States and the states of Western Europe in size and degree of military and economic autonomy. Western Europe's need for cooperation and supranational organization is therefore so much more urgent than America's that the proximate goal should be a European federal union comparable in population and power to the United States.

But the unification of Western Europe would not be at the expense of the larger Atlantic unity. Consolidation on the two levels would be complementary, although phased differently in time. Indeed, the unification of Western Europe is thought of as a political precondition of the larger unity, because it would remove the impediment of America's superior power. European unity is said to be necessary, too, to bring Europe's capabilities and sense of its own interests up to a global scale, so that Europe will be able to stand alongside America in the great common tasks of containing Communist China, of coping with growing disorder in the Third World, and of economic development. As President Kennedy said in the statement later dubbed [1] his Grand Design,

We do not regard a strong and united Europe as a rival but as a partner. To aid its progress has been the basic object of our foreign policy for 17 years. We believe that a united Europe will be capable of playing a greater role in the common defense, of responding more generously to the needs of poorer nations, of joining with the United States and others in lowering trade barriers, resolving problems of currency, and commodities, and developing coordinated policies in all other economic, diplomatic, and political areas. We see in such a Europe a partner with whom we can deal on a basis of full equal-

[1] By Joseph Kraft in *The Grand Design* (New York: Harper, 1962).

ity in all the great and burdensome tasks of building and defending a community of free nations.[2]

This functionalist way of thinking about the Atlantic polity assumes that certain objective, functional problems arising from the military and economic interdependence of the Atlantic or Western European nations will compel an increasingly cooperative and ultimately a supranational solution.[3] The literature on Atlantic affairs abounds with statements about the common military and economic "needs," "tasks," "requirements," or "responsibilities" of the Atlantic peoples which can be met only if there is a European union and an Atlantic partnership. The implication is that the functional problems have the inherent power to impose the desired solution—first growing cooperation, then Atlantic partnership, then perhaps Atlantic union. Sometimes this is supposed to happen almost unconsciously, behind the backs of the governments, by virtue of the "expansive logic" of the integration process. Sometimes it is assumed to work because the needs are so apparent to any rational mind that the nations are bound to see their common interest in closer cooperation and, ultimately, in political union.

Such functionalist thinking is apolitical. It assumes (implicitly, at least) that political obstacles to the integrative process are provisional and must in time be overcome by the force of the common interest. Thus the thorny issues of a functional-political character which now divide the Atlantic allies —such as who makes alliance strategy and possesses nuclear weapons; who decides how much the supply of reserve assets

---

[2] Address entitled, "A Declaration of Interdependence," Philadelphia, July 4, 1962, *The New York Times,* July 5, 1962.

[3] An early statement of the essential ideas and programs of functionalism as applied to international relations may be found in E. H. Carr, *Nationalism and After* (New York: Macmillan, 1945). A summary statement of the functionalist theory of international integration may be found in Ernst B. Haas, *Beyond the Nation State: Functionalism and International Organization* (Stanford University Press, 1964), p. 47–50.

should grow and how it should be distributed; who has primary responsibility for correcting payments imbalances; who decides what trade discrimination is allowable; who, in other words, *defines* the common interest and *determines* the common policy—will be settled, first in a cooperative and then in a supranational manner, because the urgent need to do so will make agreement seem imperative to all. Further, and still more dubiously, it assumes that the more strictly political conflicts among nations (those which are not amenable to rational compromise based on the test of functional efficiency or economic equity), such as who leads and who follows, who is subordinate to whom, and the ever-present, touchy issues of national dignity and prestige, will also yield to the common need to work together.

In the early postwar years the facts of the Atlantic relationship seemed consistent with this functionalist and apolitical interpretation. The optimism of this way of thinking was congenial to the American temperament and its rationalist, Utopian flavor attractive to American idealism. Today, however, it is apparent that the military problems of the Alliance are not so urgent as to compel more cooperation, let alone more integration. Conflict over economic policy, too, is growing, not declining.

In short, the common Atlantic or European interests which interdependence creates lack the clarity, the precision, the urgency, and the compulsive force which are often attributed to them. Common interests have not and will not annul political conflict, although they alter its character and soften its spirit. Still less do they create a situation in which the most probable way the political structure of the West will adapt to military and economic interdependence is by the transfer of political authority to supranational organs. Considerations of functional efficiency and equity are insufficient to bring about so revolutionary a shift in political loyalty. Alliance and cooperation, if far from perfect, have proved to be enough.

The last quarter century has witnessed a deep change in the character of international politics in the Atlantic region. There has been an adaptation of the nation-state system which leaves sovereignty where it was but renders the states more competent to deal with the new environment by systems of functional cooperation. But Americans have been mistaken in believing that these changes would gradually overcome political differences and find no resting place until they had brought into being a colossal new federal state or states, European or Atlantic. Although their relationships and even their own characters have changed, the actors in the Atlantic drama are still the national states, with their different traditions, situations, goals, and visions of the future. Their political relations will continue to be a complex mixture of conflict and cooperation, whose outcome is problematic. Such, at any rate, is the thesis of this essay.

This book, then, is about the internal politics of the Atlantic Community in the 1960s, about what holds the Atlantic nations together and what divides them. The subject matter is given shape by Atlantic military and economic interdependence and by the systems of military and economic cooperation which have grown up since 1945. What holds the Atlantic states together in their military concerns is Western Europe's interest in American military protection and America's interest in Europe's military security. What holds them together in their economic concerns is a common need to manage trade and monetary relations so as to preserve or increase economic integration. What principally divides them in military matters is the question of strategy for the Alliance and who is to control the nuclear deterrent, the principal instrument of Atlantic security in a nuclear age. What divides them in their economic interests are conflicts about objectives and control of the principal instrumentalities—monetary arrangements; trade and currency barriers.

Running through and beneath these functional-political

questions are more strictly political issues. They have to do not simply with the control of military or economic instrumentalities but with ultimate questions of political power among the Atlantic nations—questions, that is, of leadership and subordination. These issues may be described in several ways. We see them as a drama of political ideas. (By "ideas" we mean not something imaginary or abstract but a powerful tendency or purpose which seeks to realize or maintain itself in actuality.)

One such tendency is the Atlantic idea. The Atlantic idea holds that the cohesion of the entire group of Atlantic nations should be the principal objective of the nations' policies. Atlantic cohesion should take precedence over the cohesion of any lesser grouping. Implicitly, at least, the Atlantic idea calls for continuation of America's position of superior power and leadership in the Atlantic Community, on the ground that it is essential for Atlantic cohesion. Some "Atlanticists" hold that American leadership ought to continue indefinitely, and that the idea of European unity is therefore inconsistent with the Atlantic idea. The official U.S. version of the Atlantic idea, however, holds that the need for American leadership is temporary and that leadership will give way to equal partnership when Europe has united. Still another version of the Atlantic idea looks beyond leadership and partnership to an Atlantic federal union as the final stage of Atlantic unification.

The other tendency is the European idea. The European idea holds that the uinfication of Europe has priority both in time and in importance over the cohesion of the Atlantic Community as a whole. The theme of the European idea is European identity and autonomy, and a rejection of indefinite American leadership as inequitable, damaging to Europe's self-respect, and inconsistent with Europeans' right to shape their own political destiny. The classical version of the European idea holds that Western Europe should unify itself by supranational means, so as to be able to wield military and economic power substantially equal to America's. Then Europe and America will be able to cooperate effectively in an equal partnership.

The classical European idea and the official American version of the Atlantic idea are thus in harmony. But other versions of the European idea hold that the purpose of European union and autonomy is not partnership with the United States but to enable Europe to pursue its own separate purposes. Potentially, at least, this version of the European idea is in conflict with the Atlantic idea. This is the sort of "Europeanism" that President de Gaulle advocates. His aim is not Atlantic partnership but to rid Europe of American political influence, so that Europe may go its own way. The Gaullist "Europe" also differs from the classical European idea in its opposition to supranationalism.

It is characteristic of Atlantic politics in the 1960s that none of these tendencies—not even the Gaullist version of the European idea—is essentially nationalistic, for all of them have to do with the political organization of a community or communities which are wider than national. The conflict, actual or potential, between the Atlantic and European ideas does not express a simple struggle for power among nations, or between the United States and a European grouping. Europeans and Americans may be found on all sides of the issues. It is rare, for example, to find a continental European concerned with foreign affairs who is not, in some degree at least, an "Atlanticist," a "European," and a "Gaullist." It would be almost as accurate to speak of the issue between the Atlantic and European ideas as one between parties or factions which cross national lines as to call them conflicts of national interests. They partake of both.

The most important political struggles of this troubled century have not been peripheral conflicts among nations in the nineteenth century manner. They have been systemic, ideological conflicts among national states as actors in and constituents of wider than national political systems. Their struggles have not been simply about the interests and power of the separate nations but about the political organization and the ideological tendency of the wider systems. In this sense the nature of Atlantic politics in the 1960s reflects the nature of contemporary international politics generally. But the cohesion of the Atlantic nations makes Atlantic politics in the 1960s quite different from the politics of Europe in the 1930s, or the politics of the global political system today.

Our aim, then, is to explore this new sort of international politics in the particular form it takes within the Atlantic Community. There is an element of arbitrariness in focusing on the internal politics of the Atlantic world in abstraction from its external environment. We believe that this abstraction is justified by the special character of Atlantic political relations. This essay is analytical rather than prescriptive. Along the way a number of suggestions about American policy are made, but they are intended to illustrate the analysis rather than to define a comprehensive Atlantic policy for the United States.

CHAPTER ONE

The Atlantic Alliance in a Nuclear Age

Recent discussion of the Atlantic relationship has been preoccupied with the "disarray" of the Atlantic Alliance. Pessimism about its future is the current mood. Indeed, if the standard of comparison is the Alliance in its early years, or the expectations of orthodox Atlantic doctrine, the state of the Alliance is disheartening. Yet if the standard were more realistic, perhaps the conclusion would be more hopeful.

True, the Alliance has failed to fulfill earlier hopes, and the attitudes of the allies toward it are less positive than they were. But dissension among the allies does not necessarily mean that the convergence of their basic security interests is in jeopardy. The important question is whether changes in attitudes and in the objective military situation have reduced fundamentally Western Europe's need for American protection or America's stake in Europe's security.

In the contemporary debate about the Alliance this question has in fact been raised. The growth of Soviet nuclear power, it is said, has affected critically the deterrent effect of the American guarantee. It is asserted, further, that the Western European nations now possess collectively the resources to mount a nuclear deterrent of their own adequate to deter a Soviet Union which has learned the need of military caution in a nuclear age. Some Europeans feel that Europe not only can but should create its own autonomous capacity to deter the Soviet Union, not simply in order to make deterrence more effective but because it is unworthy and restrictive of Europe's freedom of action to go on indefinitely depending for security on the United States.

Still more radically, it has been contended that nuclear weapons and domestic evolution have so altered Soviet objectives that peace in Europe could now be maintained, without the need for antagonistic coalitions, by a European security arrangement in which the United States and the Soviet Union would simply guarantee all European frontiers against attack from any quarter.

We shall consider these contentions presently. First, however, it is necessary to have a closer look at the interests of the Atlantic allies in the Alliance—the benefits it brings them and the burdens it imposes—as affected by changes in the general strategic situation.

From Balance of Power to Balance of Terror

We begin with two facts as strange as they are familiar. One is the nuclear stalemate. The other is the longevity of the Atlantic Alliance.

Early in the nuclear age it was thought that the advantage of the offensive in war had so increased that the temptation to a powerful and expansionist state armed with nuclear weapons might prove irresistible. In practice, nuclear weapons have had the opposite effect. Because their power to destroy is so enormous, and because the virtual certainty of retaliation would visit upon the aggressor destruction far in excess of anything possibly to be gained by attack, nuclear weapons have made possible a remarkable military stability in the zone of direct confrontation of the two great powers, despite their intense political and ideological rivalry. The result is a degree of military stability Europe has not known since 1900. In this time of technological weapons and ideological wars, peace by balance of nuclear terror has unexpectedly proven to be more stable than peace by balance of conventional military power.

The military stability in Europe is matched by the stability of the means by which it has been achieved, the Atlantic Alliance.

In the early postwar years the general assumption on both sides of the Atlantic was that America's military involvement in Western Europe would not last long. In 1944 President Roosevelt had told Prime Minister Churchill that America would be out of Europe within two years after the end of the war. His prognosis seemed to be confirmed by the precipitate American demobilization after V-J Day. At first Americans assumed, in Wilsonian fashion, that peace in Europe would be maintained, not by American participation in a European balance of power, but by "collective security" and the cooperation of the permanent members of the UN Security Council.[1] A few years later, when the measure of the war's toll in Europe had been taken and Stalin had proved himself no Wilsonian, the United States committed itself firmly (first in the Vandenburg Resolution and then in the North Atlantic Treaty) to maintain European security against Russia. It was still generally assumed, however, that the American commitment and military presence would last only until the Western European states recovered and again assumed the normal responsibility of sovereign powers for their own security.

[1] "As the provisions of the four-nation declaration [concerning the establishment of a general international organization based on the principle of sovereign equality of all peace-loving states] are carried into effect," said Secretary of State Cordell Hull in 1944, "there will no longer be need for spheres of influence, for alliances, for balance of power, or any other of the special arrangements through which, in the unhappy past, the nations strove to safeguard their security or to promote their interests." "Bases of the Foreign Policy of the United States," *Department of State Bulletin*, March 25, 1944, p. 276.

There was, of course, nothing remarkable in this assumption. What is remarkable is that today, more than twenty years after V-E Day, with recovery long since complete, Western Europe is still largely dependent for its security on American power. Surely it is without precedent that 250 million talented people, with a rapidly growing industrial economy, who in World War II had more than 20 million men under arms, who outrank the Soviet Union in every material measure of military potential except land area, nevertheless depend for their security on the guarantee of an ally three thousand miles away.

In the century preceding World War I peace was maintained in Europe—fairly successfully considering the rivalry of the European powers—by the deterrent effect of a balance of military power. Unlike the present bipolar balance, the classical European balance of power was a multipolar system. The five great powers of the day did not form politically cohesive and lasting alliances such as the Atlantic Alliance and the Warsaw Pact. Their alignments were temporary and shifting arrangements directed now against this, now against that rival. The system was not always successful in preventing war. But the European wars between 1815 and 1914 were limited and short, and they left the political and territorial status quo ante bellum only marginally changed. The relative success of this system in keeping the peace and preventing drastic political change earned it the name of the Concert of Europe.

Two of the principal reasons which explain the classical European system are relevant to this inquiry. One was political: the positive objectives of the powers were limited to minor territorial or strategic gains. Their rivalry was not ideological; no nation sought to alter fundamentally the political or constitutional structure of Europe. A second reason was that the military means available to the powers—small professional armies and navies—were as limited as their ends. The support in peacetime of the forces necessary to maintain the balance of power was not beyond the nations' limited resources and fiscal means, but they lacked both the will and the means to achieve imperial dominion or hegemony in Europe. Thus the powers were content to play power politics as though it were a game of poker with a low limit on bets and with the understanding that no major player would lose more than he could afford.

The system broke down in this century when military means ceased to be so limited and when the political objectives of ambitious powers became ideological and total. War, which in Europe after 1815 had been an affair of small professional armies and navies, became in this century a protracted and total struggle of attrition between mass armies of conscripts, with entire national economies mobilized. The change in military means was matched by the change in political ends. Ideological nationalism of an intensity previously unknown made its appearance during World War I. In Germany and Italy nationalism combined in the 1930s with nihilistic, atavistic, revolutionary ideologies whose political objectives went far beyond traditional considerations of national advantage. France and Britain found it politically impossible until too late to take seriously these irrational, repulsive creeds and the dictators' outrageous political aims. Moreover, preparation in peacetime for total war was far more expensive, absolutely and relative to national income and fiscal capacity, than the maintenance of forces of the nineteenth-century sort. The pacific democracies were reluctant, or found it impossible for domestic reasons, to maintain in peacetime forces adequate to maintain the military balance on which peace depended. Indeed, by the late 1930s it might have required something close to permanent mobilization in France and Britain to deter Hitler.

Nor were the extra-European powers, the United States and the Soviet Union willing or politically able to help maintain a European military balance. The United States, isolationist, traditionally aloof from "Europe's quarrels," with a tiny peacetime army, did not judge its security to be directly threatened by Hitler's rising power and France and Britain's weakness until too late. The Soviet Union was too hostile to the West on ideological grounds to play a reliable role in the European balance, as Stalin's cynical and nearly suicidal pact with Hitler demonstrated.

The decisions of the United States in 1945 to stay in Europe and, in 1949, to conclude its first peacetime alliance, were in the main a response to the power vacuum in Western and Central Europe into which an ambitious and hostile Soviet Union seemed sure to move if not deterred. The situation was essentially different than it had been in 1918 when, though there was also a power vacuum in Central and Eastern Europe, no aggressive state hostile to the United States existed to take advantage of it.

But if the initial Soviet threat to a prostrate Europe explains the origin of the Atlantic Alliance, it hardly explains the stable European peace which the Alliance has brought, despite Russia's hostile and far-from-limited political goals. On prewar experience, one would not have anticipated that so tense and ideological a confrontation would have had this outcome. Nor does the origin of the Alliance explain its longevity. For an explanation of these novel and unanticipated features of the present political-strategic situation we must look to the effect of nuclear weapons.

The advent of nuclear weapons has made the problem of the United States and its Atlantic allies in deterring Soviet aggression today very different—and substantially easier—than was the problem of the Western democracies in the 1930s. For nuclear weapons change drastically the potential aggressor's calculus of costs and benefits. Of what value the seizure of West Berlin or even the whole of West Germany if the cost may be the destruction of organized society in the Soviet Union?

This far-reaching implication of nuclear weapons has only gradually been accepted. In the early years of the Atlantic Alliance, nuclear deterrence was too new and too untested to be quite believable. In retrospect we can see that from 1945 until well into the 1950s, America's nuclear monopoly or effective preponderance gave Western Europe a security which was well-nigh absolute. That was not, however, the estimate at the time. The Communist aggression against South Korea in 1950 was generally thought in the West to signal "the opening of a new and more militant worldwide policy. Apprehension was aroused about the possibility of other attacks: if, as some thought, Korea was to be regarded as a diversionary feint, then aggression might be expected against Iran, Yugoslavia, or Western Europe." [2]

This alarming view of Soviet intentions led to European rearmament and to a build-up of NATO's conventional forces for the purpose of creating a balance of conventional military power in Europe, on the theory that the Soviet Union might not be sufficiently deterred by the American nuclear threat alone. To be sure, the belief in an imminent Soviet invasion did not persist, and the actual build-up of NATO's conventional forces fell far short of the agreed goals. Yet throughout the 1950s NATO's strategic posture remained an ambiguous compromise between the goal—largely unrealized—of a conventional balance in Europe and the reality that Europe's security depended on the American nuclear guarantee, with conventional forces serving only the modest functions of "screen" and "trip wire." [3]

Soviet acceptance of the reality of the nuclear stalemate has apparently also been gradual. In the 1940s and early 1950s Soviet military doctrine followed Stalin's formulation in discounting nuclear weapons and stressing the role of mass

[2] Marshall D. Shulman, *Stalin's Foreign Policy Reappraised* (Cambridge, Massachusetts: Harvard University Press, 1963), p. 140.

[3] See, for example, Robert E. Osgood, *NATO, the Entangling Alliance* (University of Chicago Press, 1962), Chs. 4 and 5.

armies conventionally armed, as in World War II.[4] To be sure, Stalin did not capitalize on his conventional military preponderance in Europe, and in retrospect it may be doubted that he ever intended to. But it is by no means clear that American nuclear weapons played the decisive part in deterring him; it may have been his healthy respect for America's massive potential to fight a conventional war of attrition. Stalin's authoritative restatement in 1946 of Lenin's doctrine of inevitable war between the socialist and the capitalist powers [5] remained the official ideological position until 1956.

Soviet policy in Europe today, however, seems to accept the reality of mutual deterrence and nuclear stalemate. Khrushchev's epochal statement in February 1956 implying that nuclear weapons make Lenin's doctrine irrelevant to war between the great nuclear powers [6] has been repeated and elaborated in the course of the Sino-Soviet ideological debate.[7] Contemporary Soviet military doctrine seems to discount the possibility of using Russia's superiority in conventional forces to

[4] Raymond L. Garthoff, *Soviet Strategy in the Nuclear Age* (New York: Praeger, 1962), Ch. 4 and p. 156.

[5] Joseph V. Stalin, "New Five Year Plan for Russia," Election address delivered over radio, Moscow, U.S.S.R., February 9, 1946, *Vital Speeches of the Day*, vol. XII, No. 10, March 1, 1946, p. 300.

[6] As First Secretary Khrushchev said, "War is not a fatalistic inevitability. Today there are mighty social and political forces possessing formidable means to prevent the imperialists from unleashing war and, if they try to start it, to give a smashing rebuff to the aggressors and frustrate their adventurist plans." Report of the Central Committee of the Communist party of the Soviet Union to the Twentieth Congress, delivered by First Secretary of the Central Committee on February 14, 1956, in Paul E. Zinner, ed., *Documents on American Foreign Relations, 1956* (New York: Harper, for the Council on Foreign Relations, 1957), p. 192.

A joint statement by Khrushchev, Bulganin, and Nehru on December 13, 1955, on the occasion of the Russian leaders' visit to India, seems to have been the first public statement recognizing the reality of the nuclear stalemate. *The New York Times*, December 4, 1955.

[7] "We Communists believe that the idea of Communism will ultimately be victorious throughout the world, just as it has been victorious in our country, in China and in many other states. . . . *The main thing is to keep to the positions of ideological struggle, without resorting to arms in order to prove that one is right.* The point is that with military techniques what they are today, there are no inaccessible places in the world. Should a world war break out, no country will be able to shut itself off from a crushing blow." Nikita S. Khrushchev, "On Peaceful

win a war in Europe. The Russians seem to assume that European hostilities would tend to escalate to general nuclear war,
because the NATO allies would probably resort to nuclear
weapons.[8] Against this doctrinal background, the facts that
the Soviet combat forces in Eastern Europe have been substantially reduced, that they have been armed with tactical
nuclear weapons, and that the Russians have set in place 750
or more nuclear missiles targeted on Western Europe and
capable of covering every city and important military target
there,[9] lend support to the view that the main purpose of Soviet
military policy in Europe is not aggression or military pressure
but nuclear deterrence.

In these circumstances the debate about Soviet "intentions" and whether or not Russia has "changed," which has
preoccupied the West, has lost a great deal of its military interest. If militarily Russia is as much on the defensive as the
West, her leaders' ideological convictions and political ambitions are no longer so immediately relevant to the security of
the West, at least as long as the United States continues credibly to guarantee the security of its Atlantic allies.

Time—time in which to grasp the meaning of the destructive power of modern weapons; time to see their effect on the
adversary's way of thinking; time to observe his caution in
major crises which could have unleashed nuclear war—has
gradually changed a tense and seemingly inflammable confrontation into a stable stalemate in which the advantage of
military stability outweighs, for both great powers, the frustration of political and ideological hopes. In this limited sense the

---

Coexistence," *Foreign Affairs*, October 1959, reprinted in Philip E. Mosely, ed.,
The Soviet Union 1922–1962: A Foreign Affairs Reader (New York: Praeger,
for the Council on Foreign Relations, 1963), p. 403. (Italics in original.)

"In our day there are only two ways: peaceful coexistence or the most destructive war in history. There is no third choice." Same, p. 405.

[8] Raymond Aron, *Paix et Guerre* (Paris: Calmann-Lévy, 1962), p. 421; Garthoff, cited, p. 104.

[9] See Alastair Buchan, "The Balance of Power," *Defence, A Financial Times
Survey*, London, March 23, 1964, p. 17.

cold war in Europe is now history—not because the great powers have ceased to be rivals and even enemies, but because they have withdrawn psychologically a safe distance from the brink of the abyss; because both sides understand the awful weapons which have so paradoxically brought reliable peace. Mutual deterrence works.

Nuclear Parity and the American Guarantee

There is, nevertheless, still something fantastic about the notion of a stable peace based on a threat of mutual suicide. Despite the evidence that a stalemate in Europe exists and the belief that its continuation is in the interest of both great powers, doubts about its stability remain. They arise from the presumed effect of growing Soviet nuclear power, and the increasing invulnerability of the Soviet delivery system, on the credibility of the American guarantee.

As Russia's "second-strike capability" grows, it is said, the will of the United States to make good on its nuclear guarantee of Western Europe will weaken. Inevitably, the credibility of the American threat to strike Russia if she moves against America's European allies must decline, and with the deteriorating credibility of the guarantee, deterrence may break down. It is one thing to say (the argument continues) that nuclear weapons in the hands of a satisfied and relatively pacific democracy, the United States, kept the peace in Europe when America's nuclear preponderance was so great as to preclude Soviet retaliation.[10] It is quite another to be convinced that the achievement by the Soviet Union of the capacity to kill Americans "in the tens of millions" (Secretary of Defense Mc-

---

[10] Strategic stability in the days of America's nuclear monopoly or effective "counterforce" capability seems to have been the result not only of America's defensive political posture but also of what has been called "nuclear self-deterrence." The power of nuclear weapons is so disproportionate that the United States (and perhaps the Soviet Union also) is inhibited from using them, even against a power unable to retaliate, by a deep moral anxiety compounded with the vague fear that if the taboo against using nuclear weapons were to be violated, the eventual consequences for international order might be incalculably serious.

Namara's words) even after absorbing the first nuclear blow does not materially alter the stability of the balance.

The facts about the growth of Soviet strategic nuclear forces and their increasing invulnerability are now fairly clear. "In my statement a year ago," said Secretary of Defense Robert McNamara in 1963, "I pointed out that 'as the Soviet Union hardens and disperses its ICBM force and acquires a significant number of missile-launching submarines (as we must assume that they will do in the period under discussion) our problem will be further complicated.' There is increasing evidence that this is the course the Soviet Union is following. . . . A very large increase in the number of fully hardened Soviet ICBM's and nuclear-powered ballistic missile-launching submarines would considerably detract from our ability to destroy completely the Soviet strategic nuclear forces. It would become increasingly difficult, regardless of the form of the attack, to destroy a sufficiently large proportion of the Soviet's strategic nuclear forces to preclude major damage to the United States, regardless of how large or what kind of strategic forces we build. . . ." [11]

The weight of expert opinion seems to be that the balance of strategic power is likely to become more nearly equal over the next decade. The number of Soviet "hardened" strategic missiles and missile-launching submarines is expected to grow, and there is evidence that the United States will slacken its efforts to add to the size of its strategic forces. "There is . . . the prospect of the emergence of a kind of *de facto* parity by 1970—an effective parity because of the invulnerability of the forces, however unequal, on both sides." [12]

[11] Statement of Secretary of Defense Robert S. McNamara before the House Armed Services Committee entitled, "The Fiscal Year 1964–65 Defense Program and 1964 Defense Budget," January 30, 1963, pp. 29–30. There are similar statements in the Secretary's statement before the same committee on January 27, 1964, pp. 29–32.

[12] Edmund Stillman and Anthony J. Wiener, in collaboration with Francis E. Armbuster and David A. Robison, *European Defense, American Interests and the Prospects for NATO,* a report prepared for the Atlantic Policy Studies of the Council on Foreign Relations by the Hudson Institute, Harmon-on-Hudson, New York, March 30, 1964 (mimeographed), p. 40.

Some analysts have not hesitated to draw from the approach of nuclear parity the conclusion that alliances, including the Atlantic Alliance, are obsolete. "In the face of an adversary armed with weapons of mass destruction," says General Pierre Gallois, "military alliances have become singularly precarious. If it is scarcely credible that a government would risk annihilation in trying to protect its own highest interests, it is difficult to conceive that it would take similar risks for the benefit of another country, even if that country is an ally." [13] Professor Hans Morgenthau and others have stated the same thesis in more uncompromising terms.[14] By this logic there is in a nuclear age an absolute distinction between deterring an attack on one's own territory and on the territory of an ally. The fate of the Atlantic Alliance is therefore to separate or to federate. There can be no middle course.

Such reasoning is unconvincing because it treats the question of the credibility of a military guarantee by one state to another, which common sense tells us is a matter of degree, in absolute, black-and-white terms. The promise of a guarantor to come to the aid of his ally if attacked is credible or incredible to a potential aggressor depending on a number of considerations. One is the real value of the security of the ally to the guarantor: his stake in the success of deterrence. (In the case of the Atlantic Alliance, the American stake in Western Europe's security is very high, as we shall see presently.) Another is the effective power of the guarantor to punish the aggressor, which is not here in question. Still another is the seriousness of the commitment, as evidenced by the words of the

---

[13] *Le Monde Diplomatique,* April 1963, quoted in Ronald Steel, *The End of Alliance* (New York: The Viking Press, 1964), p. 35. General Gallois is credited with having first developed in systematic form the argument that nuclear weapons may make military alliances obsolete, at least as to alliances of deterrence against a great nuclear power. His argument is fully stated in his major work, *The Balance of Terror: Strategy for the Nuclear Age* (Boston: Houghton Mifflin, 1961).

[14] Hans Morgenthau, "The Crisis in the Western Alliance: An American View," *Commentary,* March 1963, p. 187. Similar views are expressed by Ronald Steel, cited, Ch. 3.

treaty and by symbolic acts such as the stationing of the guarantor's troops on the ally's soil. In these respects, too, the Atlantic commitment seems solid.

Important also, especially in a nuclear alliance, is the guarantor's will and ability to create a situation in which, in the event of aggression, his response might be taken out of his hands by the momentum of military and psychological events. This is the "trip-wire" function of the American troops in Germany, which differs from their symbolic function as an earnest of the commitment. For their presence close to the Iron Curtain means that American blood would be shed the moment Germany were attacked. Even if Moscow were at pains to make clear that the aggression was local and limited in aim, the direct involvement of American troops would tend to involve the United States emotionally, increasing for the aggressor the risk that the guarantee would be honored. Tactical nuclear weapons in the hands of NATO's front-line divisions in Germany add further to the aggressor's risk, since the presence of such weapons is now generally thought to increase the risk of escalation to strategic (general) nuclear war.

Thus the situation in which the Soviet Union has to make a decision whether to attack in Europe or to be deterred includes important symbolic, material, and psychological elements tending to increase the risk that the American guarantee would be honored, if not wholly deliberately, at least through a process of escalation passing beyond Washington's control. This is not to deny that the approach of nuclear parity between the great powers has *some* effect on the credibility of the American guarantee, but the effect is not necessarily critical; parity is one factor among others.

Like new weapons systems in the past, weapons of mass destruction change the quantitative terms in which a potential aggressor makes his calculus of risk versus potential benefit. But nuclear weapons do not change the nature of the calculus. A potential aggressor must consider today, as in the past, two questions. One is the probability that the guarantor will act in accordance with his commitment; the other is the amount of injury which the aggressor would incur if the commitment were carried out. It is the mathematical product, so to speak, of the probability and the amount of injury which the aggressor must weigh against the value of what he hopes to gain by aggression.

As compared with a situation in which the guarantor alone has a large strategic nuclear capability, the effect of nuclear parity is to reduce the probability that the guarantor will carry out his threat if the aggressor attacks. But if the alliance has been established with sufficient solemnity, and if the guarantor has managed to create a situation in which the chance of escalation to all-out nuclear war is, or seems to be, real, the aggressor's risk is nevertheless too great, given the enormous damage he would incur if the guarantee were fulfilled. As long as there is, in the view of the potential aggressor, even a very small probability that the guarantor's threat will be carried out, he is unlikely to take the chance.

It may seem that nuclear deterrence in a situation of parity is only a colossal bluff. Is not the risk of national suicide involved in the mutual threats the same for the guarantor as for the aggressor? If only the aggressor can summon the nerve, can he not call the bluff and move at will against the guarantor's non-nuclear ally? For then, indeed, the guarantor's threat will have become an incredible threat to commit suicide. But this argument is fallacious because it assumes the very point at issue: whether the aggressor will *dare* to call the "bluff." Abstractly it may be true that the aggressor's statistical chances of getting away with it are good, at least if he keeps his aims limited. Yet who but a madman would take such a gamble even on favorable odds, when the price of error is his nation's life—*especially* where his aims are limited? [15]

[15] As Raymond Aron explains, "If one begins with the hypothesis that aggression has taken place (Paris bombed but the Soviets have promised to spare Washington), one may justifiably conclude that there will be no American intervention, but

The situation of the United States as a guarantor of its European allies is, then, quite different from that of the Soviet Union in the hypothetical role of would-be aggressor. The United States, because it is on the defensive, need not make the first move. It need not make the fateful decision to take the first risk of initiating thermonuclear war. Nuclear deterrence inhibits the aggressor more than the defender. Weapons of mass destruction give to nations on the diplomatic defensive, whose leaders are willing to make an unequivocal commitment to allies in whose security they have a large and obvious stake, an incomparable power to deter military aggression even by a rival comparably armed. Rather than being obsolete, some *defensive* alliances are more effective for deterrence than they were when weapons were less destructive and the risks of aggression were correspondingly more proportionate to the potential gains. In the nuclear age, Von Clausewitz's dictum that defense is the stronger form of war acquires new meaning.

Indeed, the American guarantee protects not only the European allies but the Western European neutrals as well. Again, the gain to the aggressor would not be worth the risk, even though the risk is less by reason of the absence of a formal guarantee. For it must be obvious to the Soviet Union that

---

if one begins with the hypothesis that the American threat has been made with the necessary solemnity, one may conclude that there will be no aggression. The whole question depends on one's starting point. Personally, it seems to me that the starting point which common sense demands is the situation as it now presents itself to the two Great Powers: as long as one or the other does not take the initiative to provoke his rival, he is sure of avoiding the horrors of thermonuclear war. Since these horrors are disproportionately great, it is sufficient to create a risk, even a slight risk, to cause the Great Power, however ambitious for conquest one may suppose it to be, to prefer to abstain (so long as the abstention does not put the Great Power itself in peril). Because aggression is too irrational to occur, the party on the defensive will not be forced to . . . choose between capitulating and executing his thermonuclear threat. . . . In the case of a dialogue between the two Great Powers, thermonuclear weapons are employed defensively only; each power brandishes them to prevent certain initiatives by the other, neither brandishes them to cover its own aggression and to prevent the other from defending positions of the first order." Cited, pp. 426–7.

the NATO allies might not stand by while Sweden, for example, were threatened or attacked. The Western military reaction which might ensue would contain the seeds of general nuclear war. The value to the Soviet Union of defeating and occupying Sweden would hardly be worth that risk. (This is not, of course, to suggest that since the neutrals are secure without an alliance, the Atlantic Alliance can therefore be dispensed with. The act of withdrawing the American guarantee would increase the danger of Soviet aggression because it would be a clear signal to the Soviet Union that American concern for Western Europe's security had diminished radically.)

The approach of nuclear parity between the great powers does have important implications for the Atlantic Alliance. But its effects are mainly *within* the Alliance. It tends to divide the allies because it impinges unevenly on their strategic and political concerns. For the United States, now that it is vulnerable to Soviet nuclear weapons, the Alliance becomes increasingly a means of preventing nuclear war between the United States and the Soviet Union. For Europeans, the Alliance remains mainly a means of preventing any kind or degree of Soviet aggression or military pressure. As we shall see in the following chapter, this difference of perspective between Europeans and Americans brings to the surface latent conflicts of interest about how to keep the deterrent credible with respect to various possible levels or kinds of Soviet attack. It raises the divisive issue of who is to control the deterrent.

As between the Soviet Union and the Atlantic allies, however, the rise of Soviet strategic nuclear power does not have the extreme effects which some have attributed to it. Abstractly, it may reduce the credibility of the American guarantee. But the comparison is with a period when the United States had a nuclear monopoly, or a "counterforce" capability sufficient to prevent real damage to the United States—a situation, as it were, of excess credibility. We see no convincing evidence that the growth of Soviet power in and of itself will

impair the American guarantee in sufficient degree to undermine deterrence.

The American Stake

The Alliance, then, works. It keeps the peace in Europe.
But its success in this its main function does not wholly explain its long duration. If the Alliance endures, it must be because, for both Western Europe and the United States, the relation of benefits to costs continues to be more favorable than
it would be with any alternative security arrangement.

In the early days of the Alliance it was often said that the
American interest was to keep Western Europe's industrial
wealth and manpower out of Soviet hands. Even if the Soviet
Union had been unable to make much use of Western Europe's resources for its own military ends, their denial to the
United States would have worked a massive change in the
world military balance. Today, however, the range and destructive power of nuclear weapons have reduced the significance of Europe's economic resources and geography as a
military stake in the East-West conflict. The principal basis of
American security in a strictly military sense is strategic nuclear power. Neither European bases nor access to European
economic resources, nor even their denial to the Soviet Union,
are critical any longer to American security in this narrow
sense.

But a strictly military calculus was never the sole basis of
America's interest in Western Europe's security. The loss of
Western Europe to communism (by some combination of military pressure and subversion) would have been a disaster for
this country wholly apart from its military consequences. It is
questionable whether our kind of society could continue with
democracy destroyed in Europe and our opportunities for
economic expansion narrowed by the triumph of totalitarian
socialism there. Protecting the national security means a good

deal more than maintaining America's relative military power and territorial integrity. It also includes maintaining an external political and economic environment favorable to the existence and development of our particular way of life.

This basic interest would doubtless be enough to maintain America's concern for Western Europe's security even in the absence of modern weapons. But modern weapons give that concern greater directness and immediacy, even though they have also made it possible to protect the American continent without the aid of European bases or troops. Nuclear weapons, and more particularly America's vulnerability to Soviet strategic nuclear forces, make it essential for the United States to deter any military incident in Europe which might escalate to nuclear war. In the prenuclear world it was not irrational, if hardly wise, for the United States to stay out of the European power balance, counting on its ability to win a conventional war in Europe should one occur. In present circumstances, such an assessment would be irrational to the point of being suicidal.

America's interest in the Atlantic Alliance, then, has two aspects. One is the stake in Western Europe's security because it is America's security, at least in the long run. The other is the more immediate interest in European military stability; that is, in avoiding a power vacuum in Europe which could lead to military adventures or accidents that might escalate to general war. The second interest depends, of course, upon the first. If we could be indifferent to Europe's security, there would be no need for our military involvement there, and therefore no direct risk to us from the outbreak of hostilities in Europe. Both interests exist independently of nuclear weapons, but modern weapons alter greatly their relative importance and urgency. In conditions of nuclear stalemate and political stability in Western Europe, the Soviet threat to Western Europe's independence becomes rather remote. At the same time, the vulnerability of the United States to Soviet nuclear weapons greatly enhances the immediacy and relevance for American policy of military stability in Europe.

By maintaining its guarantee, the United States therefore adds more immediately to its security than if there were no nuclear weapons. In the 1930s the American stake in the security of the Western democracies did not appear sufficiently immediate to keep the United States directly involved in the European balance of power, despite Hitler's increasingly open challenge to the political structure of Europe. If today an American return to isolationism seems improbable, it is in the main because modern weapons have driven home the lesson of two world wars—that America's first line of defense is that which separates the European democracies from their potential enemies.

The Alliance also serves in another way the American interest in preventing nuclear war. It reduces the incentive to Europeans to have nuclear forces, national or collective, of their own. Without nuclear forces, or with only small forces such as the French and British forces will be for some years, it is extremely unlikely that any European government would dare to make a first use of nuclear weapons without prior American approval. But the condition of this state of things, relatively satisfactory to Americans, is the American guarantee. Nor are the benefits of our nuclear preponderance in the Alliance a matter of security only. For Western Europe's military dependence is the principal remaining pillar of America's position of leadership, now that Western Europe no longer depends on economic aid or on political-ideological support against Communist minorities. The value to the United States of this position of leadership, particularly with respect to Germany, will be considered in later chapters.

Modern weapons not only increase the benefits to the United States of alliance with Western Europe, they also reduce its economic cost, as compared with what the situation would be if only conventional weapons existed. For the American nuclear forces needed to back up the guarantee are very nearly the same as the forces the United States needs for its own protection. Thus the incremental cost of the guarantee is not large. We would have SAC's bombers and missiles and the Navy's Polaris submarines in nearly their present numbers whether Europe needed defending or not. We would probably have conventional forces in about the same number as now, to give evidence of a serious intent to counter non-nuclear aggression, even if there were no need to station American divisions in Germany. Recent weapons developments, especially the shift from shorter-range bombers and missiles based in Europe and the Middle East to intercontinental missiles and missile-launching submarines, have increased this effect.

Indeed, relative to the military and political benefits which the Alliance brings the United States, its economic cost is small. It is not surprising that there has been so little serious domestic questioning of the Alliance or its cost. Since the Vandenburg Resolution, American isolationism, old style, has been dead.

The European Point of View

From Western Europe's standpoint, continued reliance on the American guarantee also seems to be attractive in economic and even in political terms, although psychologically it is a good deal more problematic. It is attractive because it provides reliable security at minimum economic cost. Its political cost is also low. The European allies need not pay a high price for the American guarantee in terms of political conformity or subordination. They enjoy a high degree of political autonomy within the Alliance without incurring the economic costs or taking the military risks of reaching for nuclear independence.

Under the American nuclear guarantee, the European allies are relatively free to act autonomously, a fact not without its difficulties. Great powers have always had difficulty with lesser allies, if only because they are not free to use force or threats of force against an ally as long as the alliance is necessary. But the polycentrism of alliances in a nuclear age is something new under the sun.

The point may be clarified by imagining an Atlantic alliance against a powerful Soviet Union in a pre-nuclear world. In such a world, Western Europe would have to assume the major responsibility for its own defense; it could well afford to do so if there were no alternative. There might be a European-American alliance of some kind if the Russian threat seemed serious enough, but it would not be principally based on American military power. In the absence of nuclear weapons, the American interest in Western Europe's security would be less direct and intense, because the security of the United States would not be so immediately threatened by war in Europe. The United States would hardly be willing to bear so much of the cost of defending Europe. Moreover, if the alliance were largely an American guarantee based on American forces, our military presence on European soil would have to be very large—so large, indeed, as to be a kind of protectorate, at least in Western Germany and perhaps in other exposed countries as well. To America, a democratic nation without imperial ambition or militarist tradition, to station that many troops permanently in Europe would be unthinkable in peacetime. An American presence of this kind would be even less attractive to Europeans.

With nuclear weapons, however, the cost to the United States of guaranteeing Europe consists largely of doing what we must do anyway for our own protection. Far from involving an overwhelming American military presence in Europe, the American guarantee creates a rather remote relationship, aptly called a nuclear umbrella, under which the European allies are free to move about politically and even to move closer to the East, constrained only by the political and ideological dangers which communism and Russian power still create for democratic, capitalist regimes without adequate means of self-defense.

Only France has so far chosen to make notable use of its new opportunity. "President de Gaulle is convinced," says Henry Kissinger, "that those circumstances in which the United States might be prepared to resort to its nuclear weapons cannot be fundamentally affected by his actions. In other words, the United States commitment need not be purchased by being conciliatory and cannot be jeopardized by intransigence—within very wide limits at least." [16] No doubt De Gaulle's freedom of action would be less if other European allies, particularly Germany, were to follow his example. But Britain and Germany, because they are willing to accept American political leadership, and Germany because it is also more exposed militarily, have not done so. Whether or not the opportunity is used, however, some of the political constraints of the cold war and of the early postwar period have been loosened. The internal politics of the Atlantic Alliance are likely to show it increasingly.

Similar developments are visible across the Iron Curtain, although complicated by political and ideological factors not present in the West. [17] Polycentrism in the East is more dramatic than in the West because it reflects not only causes of the same kind as have been at work in the West, but also a vigorous and sometimes violent nationalist reaction against indirect Russian rule. Yet the emergent "national socialist" regimes of Eastern Europe still lack solid popular support (except in Yugoslavia) and therefore remain in varying degree dependent for their survival on Russian political support. In-

[16] Henry A. Kissinger, *The Troubled Partnership* (New York: McGraw-Hill, for the Council on Foreign Relations, 1965), p. 17.

[17] The term "polycentrism" is said to have been coined by the Italian Communist, Palmiro Togliatti, to describe developments in Eastern Europe, the Sino-Soviet split, and ideological diversity among Communist parties in non-Communist countries.

deed, their nationalism springs in part from a desire to make themselves more legitimate in their own people's eyes. Thus polycentrism in the East produces more serious political strains; at the same time, it may not go so far as in the West. In the East as in the West, the effect is different in each country, depending on the leaders' political aims, the degree of popular support for the regime, and the military exposure. Moscow has its Gaullist France in nationalist Rumania, or Titoist Yugoslavia.

From an American standpoint, polycentrism in the Atlantic Alliance means reduced political cohesion, "disarray," and declining effectiveness of American leadership. It is the political price America pays in terms of reduced control and prestige to maintain an alliance whose military value to the United States has grown with the growth of Soviet nuclear power. The price can be reduced by skillful diplomacy, but there is no going back to the old NATO in which the American word, the American proposal, was usually honored. The change is structural. The relative political power of Europe and America, reflecting, as it does, what the Atlantic relationship gives to and requires of each, has shifted in Europe's favor.

The Question of European Military Autonomy

Nevertheless, many Western Europeans feel a certain malaise. Citizens and governments of former great powers find great difficulty in accepting dependence indefinitely, however comfortable it may be. No wonder that Charles de Gaulle's invocation of "independence" strikes a responsive chord in many European hearts, although few are willing to accept the practical implications of his vision of a "European Europe." The trans-Atlantic tension which this feeling creates is critical for an understanding of the future of the Atlantic Community. It seems probable, nevertheless, that Europe's military dependence will persist for some years yet.

Although nuclear weapons are cheap per unit of destructive power, the absolute cost of deterrence is very large. To mount a deterrent large and invulnerable enough to be an autonomous element in the strategic balance requires the mobilization of very large economic resources—large not simply in financial and physical terms but in terms of scientific and technical manpower. For nuclear deterrence today is based on an intense, exceedingly complex, and dynamic competition of weapons research and development. "The stabilization of the Soviet-American strategic relationship has been achieved only by making the apparatus of strategic deterrence a very much more complicated and costly affair for both parties." [18] There has been, it is said, some stabilization of weapons technology as to existing strategic systems, particularly as to nuclear explosives and delivery systems. But the need to stay up with or ahead of the opposition in exploring possible new systems (anti-aircraft, anti-missile and anti-submarine systems, and space-vehicle systems, for example) continues to increase the pressure on scarce scientific and technical manpower.

It seems in consequence that only advanced industrial countries of continental dimensions are able to participate *as principals* in the strategic balance, for only superpowers command adequate resources to keep up in the technological race on which deterrence depends. If this is true, none of the European allies has an immediate alternative to dependence on the United States, so long, at least, as it is unwilling to take the military and ideological risks of becoming a neutral. Looking a little farther ahead, however, the Western European allies do have a plausible alternative, although a very difficult one: to establish a European union large enough and united enough to have a unity of will and command of resources comparable to those of the Soviet Union.

The belief that political union is Western Europe's only al-

[18] Alastair Buchan, "The Changed Setting of the Atlantic Debate," *Foreign Affairs*, July 1965, p. 578.

ternative to dependence on the American guarantee is widely accepted in the United States and Western Europe today. Nevertheless, it would be wise to reserve judgment. May this consensus not be a rationalization of the status quo? Before accepting it, therefore, we may address ourselves briefly to two questions.

One question is whether it is really true that "middle powers" of the industrial strength and technological competence of Britain, France, and Germany are unable to build, on an independent national basis (perhaps with some mutual assistance short of union), strategic deterrents adequate to deter a seemingly cautious adversary such as the Soviet Union, even though the Russians dispose of a much more powerful nuclear force. The other question is what is meant in this context by "union." How much unity would be required among a group of West European states consisting, let us say, of the members of the European Economic Community, or of the Six plus Britain, to mount an adequate autonomous deterrent?

Public and official discussion of these matters has sometimes been clouded by a failure to make two distinctions. One is the difference between the capacity of France, Britain, or Germany to build a strategic nuclear force large and invulnerable enough to have some positive deterrent effect, within the context of the Alliance, as a *supplement* to American forces; and their capacity to create nuclear forces with sufficient power and credibility to serve *autonomously* to deter an attack on their own territory, or on the territory of another West European country, if the American guarantee were withdrawn. A second and related distinction is between the capacity of France, Britain, or Germany to build a deterrent based essentially on *existing* weapons technology, and their capacity to keep up with the Soviet Union in a research and development race so far as *new* weapons systems are concerned.

There is no reason to doubt the ability of the three "middle powers" of Western Europe to create national deterrent forces which add to the over-all deterrent effect of the Alliance. Even in their present vulnerable condition, the British and French forces doubtless contribute to the Soviet Union's risk that aggression against NATO Europe would escalate to general nuclear war. For they add a little to the total nuclear capability of the Alliance, and they increase by two the numbers of governments able (in theory at least) to make a first use of nuclear weapons. As these forces become stronger and less vulnerable in the next few years, their deterrent value will presumably grow, unless they are rendered obsolete by new Soviet defensive systems.

But when their value as autonomous deterrent forces is considered, the matter is quite different. If they are to be more than a supplement to an American deterrent, one must ask how large and invulnerable the "small" force must be to deter the Soviet Union. One must assess the ability of France, Britain, or Germany to stay up with the Soviet Union in the costly technological race which would be necessary to keep their forces from obsolescence. And, finally, one must consider whether the gross difference in land area, population, and population density between any one of the European powers and the Soviet Union does not create so fundamental a disproportion in the ability of the two countries to survive an exchange of nuclear blows as to render deterrence unreliable, even if the nuclear forces of both sides are relatively invulnerable.

Certain analysts have advanced a theory of "minimum" or "proportional" deterrence to support the conclusion that a national deterrent, small relative to that of the Soviet Union, wielded by a determined European power, could be effective autonomously if it were sufficiently invulnerable.[19] The argument is that the damage which such a force could inflict on the

---

[19] Gallois, *The Balance of Terror,* cited, Ch. 3. Morgenthau, cited. For negative European views on "proportional deterrence" see Club Jean Moulin, *La Force de Frappe et le Citoyen* (Paris: Editions du Seuil, 1963), p. 60; General André Beaufre, *Dissuasion et Stratégie* (Paris: Armand Colin, 1964), Ch. 2.

Soviet Union, although not nearly so great as the damage it might receive, would nevertheless be sufficient to deter, because it would be greater than the value to the aggressor of the gain from aggression.

This logic is not implausible, but it is too abstract and leaves too much out of account. It assumes the continuing ability of the European power to maintain a nuclear force capable of inflicting severe damage on the Soviet Union. Thus, it leaves out the fact of dynamic technology. It appears, for example, that the Soviet Union is already able to develop new defensive weapons systems which could substantially limit the effectiveness of a small European strategic nuclear force.[20]

On present indications it is hard to believe that France, Britain, or Germany has, on an independent national basis, the ability to compete effectively with the Soviet Union in military research and development. Britain and France are able to build substantial nuclear forces based mainly on American technology or on an imitation of it. But it seems probable that in their ability to develop *new* systems they will fall farther and farther behind the superpowers, so long, at least, as their efforts are separate and uncoordinated.[21] This also seems to be true in related areas of science and technology.[22] A 1965

[20] "The fact that both the Soviet Union and the United States now have the technical option of installing anti-air and anti-missile systems which would provide a high degree of protection against the weapons of a small nuclear power (even though both would contemplate with the greatest reluctance the vast expense and the uncertainty of installing an anti-missile system that could provide protection against each other's forces) will tend to downgrade the serious military utility of the two European nuclear forces." Buchan, "The Changed Setting of the Atlantic Debate," cited, p. 578.

[21] For similar views, see Kenneth Waltz, "The Stability of a Bipolar World," *Daedalus,* Summer 1964, p. 898, and Alastair Buchan, "The Age of Insecurity," *Encounter,* August 1963, p. 35. A somewhat more optimistic view of the European powers' capacity in military technology is expressed by Stillman and Wiener, cited, pp. 75–76.

[22] "Already there are some industrial and scientific fields in which no power the size of Britain can any longer compete with larger rivals. Modern armaments is one, space research another, supersonic civil aircraft probably a third, and there now seems to be doubt about nuclear power," Kenneth Younger, *Changing Perspectives in British Foreign Policy* (London: Oxford University Press, for the Royal Institute of International Affairs, 1964), pp. 89–90.

report of the Organization for Economic Cooperation and Development (OECD) concludes that five Western European countries (Britain, France, Germany, Belgium, the Netherlands) were *together* using only 138,000 scientists and engineers, as against some 416,000 to 487,000 in the Soviet Union and 436,000 in the United States. In money terms, corrected for differences in unit research costs, the five European countries were *together* spending only one-third to one-half as much as the Soviet Union or the United States on research and development, civilian and military.[23] These figures suggest that Britain or France or Germany would face a virtually insuperable task if it sought to stay up with the Soviet Union in military technology on an independent national basis.

But the most serious weakness in the case for autonomous European national deterrents lies in the difference of size between the Soviet Union and the European powers. An exchange of nuclear blows, for example, between France and the Soviet Union might cripple the Soviet Union; it would destroy France. The vengeance of France against the aggressor might be terrible but it would be posthumous, whereas Russia would survive.

If no alternative means of deterrence were available, the European middle powers would doubtless build such nuclear forces as they could, which might in the event prove effective as deterrents against a militarily cautious Soviet Union. But the gross asymmetry of the mutual nuclear threats makes it unlikely that even the most autonomy-minded European state would choose voluntarily to rely exclusively or primarily on its own deterrent, *so long as any alternative means of deterrence were available,* unless the alternative involved an intolerable sacrifice of national pride and freedom of action.

If the Six members of the European Economic Community were united, and especially if Britain joined them, they would probably have a sufficient command over resources to join in time the ranks of the nuclear superpowers, although

[23] *The New York Times,* December 17, 1965.

meeting the technological requirements of that role would hardly be easy, to judge from the OECD figures cited above. It is sometimes said that even a united Western Europe would not dare strive for military autonomy because its geographical area would still be much smaller and its population much denser than that of the Soviet Union, but this is doubtful. The case is rather different from that of a single European country vis-à-vis the Soviet Union, for the disproportion in size and vulnerability to nuclear attack would be less—enough so, perhaps, to make the effort to create an autonomous deterrent seem worth while in the one case although not in the other.

To achieve the requisite command of resources, the unity of the European countries would have to be sufficiently intimate to make possible considerable national specialization and international integration of the economic and technological activities and industries most closely related to modern weaponry. Specialized agencies of a more or less supranational character might be required; for example, an authority to finance and develop on an international basis a European aerospace industry; an authority to finance and promote research of military importance. Close coordination of military budgets and procurement and of weapons research and development would also be required.

In short, to create an adequate autonomous European nuclear deterrent would require that each of the participating governments commit itself more or less irrevocably to permanent dependence upon the others for the development, manufacture, and supply of the armaments upon which their security would depend. In subsequent chapters we shall consider what such a commitment would involve politically. Here we mean only to emphasize that the ability of the European Six, or the Six and Britain, to mobilize effectively their combined military potential, since it requires national specialization and interdependence on a more or less permanent basis, depends on a far-reaching political commitment.

Doubts about the feasibility of European military autonomy are frequently expressed in terms of the problem of control of nuclear weapons. It is said, for example, that there could be no credible European deterrent unless there were a single finger on the trigger—that of the President of the United States of Europe. Often it is argued that European nuclear autonomy presupposes a supranational European government, because only a common government could effectively mobilize Europe's resources for military purposes.[24] Possibly so, but this way of reasoning puts the institutional cart before the political horse. Until Europeans are ready to make the political commitment to a common and autonomous defense it is difficult to know just how much unity of control over weapons and resources, and what kind of institutional framework, would actually be required. It seems probable that institutional forms well short of federation would suffice, if the political will were there. Before the fact, however, this cannot be known. If the political will to sacrifice national autonomy for the common defense were present, institutional problems could be overcome.

We shall consider in Chapter 5 the question of whether a politically unified Europe which is militarily on its own is likely to be established. One aspect of the question may be mentioned here: the military risk involved for Europe in the transition from reliance on the American guarantee to self-reliance. The risk is that the growth of European nuclear forces beyond a certain point might cause the United States to reconsider its guarantee, thereby exposing Western Europe to Soviet military pressure. The point at which this risk arises depends on the size of the European force and on political and psychological factors, particularly the purpose and spirit of European military autonomy as perceived by Americans.

If the United States were to withdraw its guaranteee only *after* a united Europe had created an adequate nuclear force of its own, the stability of the strategic balance might remain.

---

[24] See, for example, Alastair Buchan, "Partners and Allies," *Foreign Affairs,* July 1963, pp. 624–625.

The military danger lies in the possibility that an American decision of this kind might be taken while the European force was still inadequate, in reaction to European policies deemed contrary to American interests, for example, or on the basis of an erroneous assessment of how the Soviet Union would respond to an American withdrawal. This possibility is the greater if, as some have thought, the chief impetus toward European nuclear independence is opposition to American influence rather than the desire for closer association with the United States. If this were to be the aim and spirit of European nuclear independence, the process of separation might undermine the existing structure of security before an adequate replacement had been built.

"Our commitment to the defense of Europe is absolute and irrevocable," Senator J. William Fulbright once said, but he added, "so long as the critical decisions that lead to war or peace are not removed beyond our influence and responsibility." [25]

Many Western Europeans are anxious and some are resentful about their anomalous military dependency, but they fear the consequences of attempting to go it alone. "The European dilemma lies in this sentence: *renascent Europe moving towards unity can neither leave its fate permanently in American hands, nor can it weaken or relinquish the American guarantee of its security.* To accept the first alternative would be to give up; the second would mean vulnerability and perhaps suicide." [26]

Military autonomy, then, is a possibility for a united Western Europe, provided Europeans want it enough to take the military risk and pay the price in national sovereignty.

We conclude, then, that the convergence of European and American interests on which the Atlantic Alliance rests is

[25] *Prospects for the West* (Cambridge, Massachusetts: Harvard University Press, 1963), p. 51.
[26] Club Jean Moulin, cited, p. 119. (Italics in original.)

sufficient to justify a prediction that the Alliance will survive for some years yet. Its success in military terms, its low economic and political cost to Western Europe, its low economic cost and considerable political advantage to the United States —all these favorable factors, which reflect in part the nature of modern weapons, suggest that the Alliance in some form is likely to be with us for quite a while.

This conclusion does not preclude growing dissension among the allies. Nor does it preclude considerable change in the Alliance—even, for example, the withdrawal of France, not merely from NATO, as France is now doing, but from the Alliance itself. For France's defection would leave the guarantee of Germany and the other European allies substantially intact, and France herself would continue to be protected even as the Western European neutrals are now protected.

The conclusion rests, as we have seen, on a critical assumption: that Western Europe cannot dispense with the American guarantee unless and until it takes a long and difficult step toward political union. Whether there is any other alternative to the Alliance, such as a European security pact, will be considered in the final chapter.

De Gaulle Moves against NATO

On March 9, 1966, President de Gaulle launched his long-anticipated offensive against the North Atlantic Treaty Organization. He has made it clear that all French personnel will be withdrawn from NATO's military agencies. The Supreme Headquarters Allied Powers in Europe (SHAPE) and the NATO headquarters for Central Europe (AFCENT) will have to be moved out of France, as will the American forces there. Logistical facilities in France (air bases, communications, supply dumps, pipe lines) now under American or joint allied control may have to be turned over to French control or substitutes found or built outside France.

Such adjustments will be complex, expensive, and annoying to France's allies. In terms of military effectiveness, the result will doubtless be less satisfactory than present arrangements. In political terms, the French decision and its implementation increase the level of dissension in the Alliance. Yet the question relevant to our inquiry is whether or how much the French assault on NATO will affect the Alliance more fundamentally.

De Gaulle has been at pains to make clear that he opposes the organization, NATO, not the Alliance. "France does not intend to use the clause of the treaty of April 4, 1949, which allows any member to denounce the treaty from 1969. Consequently, the alliance shall continue as far as France is concerned." [27] Nor is the French president opposed to the North Atlantic Council, with its national delegations and subcommittees of military and political advisers; for there the allies meet as sovereign, independent states. What he opposes are the military agencies of NATO: SHAPE and its subordinate commands, including AFCENT, the most important. These agencies, organized as military headquarters, staffed by military personnel drawn from the several allies, commanded by the supreme allied commander, Europe (SACEUR), an American general, are the principal substance of the military "integration" which De Gaulle rejects.

The extent of this integration is sometimes exaggerated. NATO is often spoken of as though it were a supranational military establishment. The impression is conveyed that General Lemnitzer, now SACEUR, like Generals Norstad, Gruenther, and Eisenhower before him, is chief of staff and supreme commander of an integrated army, navy, and air force which includes all forces assigned by the allies for the defense of Western Europe. The reality is more modest. SHAPE is an international planning staff. It makes plans and estimates of

[27] French Government Statement on the North Atlantic Treaty Organization, Paris, March 9, 1966, *The New York Times,* March 10, 1966.

force requirements. But SHAPE's plans and estimates are only recommendations; they do not bind the governments.

SHAPE and its subordinate agencies are also stand-by or shadow military headquarters, to be activated in an emergency, rather than operating commands with continuous control of combat forces. With the significant exception of the military forces of the Federal Republic of Germany, SACEUR and his regional commands do not actually command the forces which the allies have formally "assigned to NATO." In peacetime the forces remain under national control. Only German forces are "integrated" in a real sense; i.e., divorced from national control. The twelve divisions and the air units of the Bundeswehr are under SACEUR's operational control. The Federal Republic has no general staff or military high command of its own.

Germany's unique position in NATO had its origin in the political problems raised by German rearmament in the 1950s and the failure of the European Defense Community (EDC) project. The EDC, it will be recalled, was France's response to the insistence of the United States on the rearmament of Germany. EDC was to have been a truly integrated, supranational European military establishment. Its purpose was to make possible a German contribution of manpower and arms to Europe's defense without a German military establishment under German control. When in 1954 the French Parliament failed to ratify the EDC Treaty, the American rejoinder was to seek a substitute by putting German forces under SHAPE's command. For Germany, rearmament on this basis was the price of ending the occupation and regaining sovereignty. Indeed, German rearmament on a strictly national basis would have been as unacceptable in Germany as elsewhere.

This arrangement remains acceptable—indeed attractive —to Germans for military and political reasons. The integration of German forces under NATO tends to keep the United States closely committed to the defense of Germany. More particularly, it makes it difficult for the United States forces in Germany to be withdrawn. For if the American forces were withdrawn or greatly reduced, the United States would be in a weak position to insist that German forces remain under NATO control. And without the reassuring American military presence, the Federal Republic might insist that its security required control of its own forces, and perhaps their armament with tactical nuclear weapons under exclusive German control. This the United States is bound to prevent, if it can, for fear of the political repercussions within the Alliance and on East-West relations. The Federal Republic is also well aware that a move to assert national control over German forces would seriously disturb Germany's neighbors. The integration of German forces under NATO is thus the *quid pro quo* for American troops, and American troops are the *quid pro quo* for German integration.

Germany in this respect (as in some others) is "less equal" than its allies. Formally and symbolically, however, Germany's status is the same as that of the other allies; for all allied forces designated for European defense are nominally subject to SHAPE. The situation is one which German leaders have been able to justify to their constituents, and no important voice has been raised in Germany against it. A few days after the French announced their intentions about NATO, Chancellor Erhard was reported to have said that any arrangement in which a German general staff and an independent German national army would be revived was unthinkable. NATO and military integration under it, he said, were "unrenounceable." "The present form of the alliance suits us to a T." [28]

As for the other European allies, France of course excepted, it seems probable that they will choose to retain NATO's present structure, as nearly as France's withdrawal permits, in view of the military and political functions it

[28] *The New York Times,* March 16, 1966.

serves. As one commentator put it, "Integration of NATO forces, including the American involvement, is the force that holds not one, but the two greatest powers on the European continent, in check: the Soviet Union, to its distress, and Western Germany with its consent."

NATO, then, seems likely to persist, but its importance should not be exaggerated. NATO is not the Alliance and the Alliance could exist without it if it had to. What protects Western Europe is American power and the American commitment, supported by the presence of U.S. forces. What holds Germany in check is the Soviet military threat and the American presence. Integration of German forces under NATO is useful and desirable because it symbolizes these underlying realities of power and commitment and renders them more acceptable to the allies, except France. It therefore adds materially to the stability of the Alliance. But it is the underlying realities, not the institutional superstructure, which are critical.

President de Gaulle knows this and therefore feels safe in weakening NATO's institutions, in the interest of increasing France's autonomy and freedom of action. But the Alliance and NATO, too, will survive De Gaulle—not unchanged or unimpaired but essentially intact, for they rest on common interests and objective realities which are beyond the reach of French policy.

CHAPTER TWO

Control of the Deterrent

In this chapter we turn our attention from what holds the Atlantic allies together in their military concerns to what divides them. Among allies, controversy is inevitable. Disagreements arise because no alliance serves equally well the interests of all the allies. For some, the benefits are bound to seem more valuable, or the burdens and risks greater, than for others. Even in wartime, when the incentive to agree is at a maximum, it is difficult to come together on political objectives, on strategy, and on the size, deployment, and coordination of forces. In peacetime it is much more so, because the allies must prepare to meet a range of hypothetical enemy actions rather than a definite military situation, and because the need to agree is less pressing.

Dissension among allies is rarely concerned with strictly military issues. Even when the argument is ostensibly technical, the political element is nearly always present. Moreover, in a situation of stalemate and nuclear parity, political issues are particularly acute and difficult to resolve. For stalemate and parity raise to prominence the thorny question of who controls the deterrent. For all the major allies, this question moves to the top of the agenda, both for reasons of security and for more strictly political reasons. We return to the control problem after a brief look at the background of strategic controversy in NATO.

Strategic Controversy in the Alliance

If for no other reason than geography, the interests of the allies in their mutual security arrangements differ. The United States, still safe from invasion, espouses strategic doctrines and deployments whose main emphasis is on preventing general war. Europeans are naturally more sensitive than Americans to the danger of limited hostilities confined to Europe. They, accordingly, propose strategies, force dispositions and weapons systems whose emphasis is deterrence of enemy action of that kind.

Controversy whose origin lies in this natural difference of security interests has existed almost from the beginning of the Alliance. At first the issue was between those who considered the Alliance a simple commitment by the United States to come to Europe's aid if attacked, and the adherents (primarily French) of a "forward strategy," who argued that it was necessary to balance Soviet conventional forces by means of a large conventional build-up in Europe. When the invasion of South Korea caused a sudden shift of the Western assessment of Soviet aggressiveness, NATO's strategic doctrine was formally revised to incorporate the "forward strategy" concept, implemented by the so-called "Lisbon goals" for the build-up of NATO's conventional forces. Nevertheless, the emphasis on the American nuclear guarantee increased, receiving its classic formulation in 1954 in Secretary of State Dulles's well-known "massive retaliation" speech.[1] In practice, the conven-

---

[1] Address by the Secretary of State before the Council on Foreign Relations, New York, January 12, 1954. *Department of State Bulletin*, XXX, January 25, 1954, pp. 107–110.

tional element of the new strategy remained largely declaratory. The implementation of the Lisbon goals was very slow. It depended on the rearmament of Germany, which was not agreed until 1954. NATO's effective strategy remained massive retaliation, somewhat qualified by the slow build-up of conventional forces whose function was essentially that of a "trip wire" to unleash a retaliatory American strategic nuclear attack.

The introduction of tactical nuclear weapons into NATO forces in Europe had the effect of increasing the stress on nuclear deterrence or massive retaliation as the basis of NATO strategy. At the time the strategic function of these new weapons was officially explained, not in terms of nuclear deterrence, but as an additional and more powerful form of artillery or tactical air support, to supplement the conventional fire power of NATO's divisions and help offset Soviet superiority in conventional forces. Their practical effect, however, was to emphasize still more the threat of massive retaliation. For the arming of front-line forces with nuclear weapons increased the risk of rapid escalation of any hostilities, conventional or not, to general war.

Throughout the 1950s Europeans remained uneasy about massive retaliation and NATO's weakness in conventional forces. Their fear was not that the strategy was inadequate to win a general war if one were fought. What they feared was that the Soviet Union would not be deterred from using its local superiority in conventional forces to overrun Western Europe, and that the United States would then be faced with the bitter choice of accepting a *fait accompli* or "liberating a corpse"—destroying its allies along with the enemy. When Soviet forces also began to acquire nuclear weapons, the fear of nuclear devastation was added to the fear of enemy occupation.

Nevertheless, Europe's uneasiness about massive retaliation did not cut deeply into the cohesion of the Alliance, in political and psychological terms. Europe still felt too immediately threatened, too dependent on American economic support, and too lacking in self-confidence to challenge American leadership and doctrine. Nor was there, in truth, any effective way in which they could do so, since they were unable or unwilling to raise the large conventional forces which their view of NATO strategy required.

As the existence of a nuclear stalemate has been accepted in the United States, as the realization has spread that a massive Soviet assault on Western Europe is unlikely and that the principal military threat to Western Europe is of limited or even accidental hostilities, the content of the strategic debate has changed. In a sense, the Americans and the Europeans have switched sides.

The United States, with its new vulnerability to Soviet weapons, now propounds a doctrine for NATO which, far from bringing immediately and automatically into play the American strategic forces in accordance with the massive retaliation strategy, requires that so far as possible, and for as long as possible, aggression should be resisted by conventional means. This strategic concept was first put forward by Secretary of Defense McNamara at a meeting of the NATO Council in Athens in 1961. He sought to speed NATO's conventional build-up and to make actual the largely declaratory conventional element of NATO strategy. American strategic thinking has become increasingly concerned with preventing rapid escalation from conventional to nuclear hostilities and therefore increasingly anxious to create the capacity to make a graduated range of response to various possible levels of Soviet attack. It has also become increasingly concerned with how to control and limit nuclear war should it break out.

Europeans, in contrast, who formerly feared the doctrine of massive retaliation and pressed for a conventional build-up, now fear that too heavy a reliance on conventional resistance may weaken nuclear deterrence and encourage Soviet adventures. They fear that America's vulnerability to Soviet nuclear weapons, reflected in the new American doctrines of "conventional pause" and "flexible response," really means that the Soviets could nip off a substantial piece of NATO territory while the United States was paralyzed by fear of Soviet nuclear retaliation. Europeans, therefore, seek to keep the United States committed to its old posture of massive retaliation. In the German view, this is to be accomplished by emphasis on the early use of NATO's tactical nuclear weapons in the event of military aggression of any substantial size. Germans reason that Soviet knowledge that tactical nuclear weapons might be used at an early stage of the battle would create fear of rapid escalation to general nuclear war. In the French view, this risk of rapid escalation is to be further increased by the existence of independent nuclear deterrents with a strategic as well as a tactical capability.

Americans and Europeans both count mainly on nuclear deterrence to safeguard Europe. Both recognize that deterrence depends on presenting the Soviet Union with an unacceptably large risk of escalation to nuclear war from even relatively minor hostilities. But at this point agreement ends, for Europeans want to maximize the risk. As the French strategic theorist General André Beaufre has put it, "It is nuclear instability which makes deterrence stable." Americans, for their part, put their emphasis on making escalation to the extremes less probable, since that is what most threatens the United States, arguing that a lesser risk of escalation is sufficient for deterrence.[2]

[2] "Because of Europe's experience [with conventional warfare], Europe is instinctively and resolutely hostile to any doctrine which, by admitting of forms of limited war, would make the unleashing of a war more probable. While the Americans, justly afraid of the threat which weighs on their continent, are led to explore the possibility of controlling conflicts to maintain their local character, the Europeans know that any conflict in Europe would open up for them unforeseeable consequences and prefer to maintain the peace of this part of the world by the

This controversy has so far proved impossible to resolve, either at the level of formal doctrine or in practice.

NATO's effective strategy, as reflected in actual force dispositions and weapons, is an ambiguous compromise between the European and the American views. On the one hand, NATO's conventional strength has considerably increased as the delayed result of the decisions made in the wake of the Korean War. On the other hand, in accordance with the decision made in 1954, these forces have been armed with tactical nuclear weapons, which greatly increases the risk of uncontrolled escalation—a fact inconsistent with a real conventional option.[3]

For the purposes of this inquiry, the military content of this controversy is less interesting than its divisive effect on the Alliance. Indeed, the lay observer cannot escape a feeling of unreality about the military issue in the terms in which it has been posed. Who knows—who can know—what degree of escalation risk is required to deter the Soviet Union? All that is surely known today is that the Russians *are* deterred, but not exactly why. As Henry Kissinger has said, "It is impossible, however, to demonstrate why something has *not* occurred. It can never be proved, for example, whether peace has been maintained because NATO pursues an optimum strategy or only a marginally effective one." [4] Indeed, for all that anyone can know, the present situation involves a large measure of

threat of a general conflict. . . . Europeans generally prefer total peace by great danger, rather than to see Europe become again a theatre of even minor operations." General André Beaufre, "Dissuasion et Stratégie," *Survival*, March–April 1965, p. 56.

[3] "Because these weapons have come to be regarded as an integral part of the division's . . . firepower, the division may become unable to fight without them. Any visitor to a field headquarters will have noted the assurance with which divisional commanders of all nationalities now assume that they would be using these weapons from the start of hostilities and that they would be helpless without them. . . ." Alastair Buchan, *The Defence of Western Europe*, Adelphi Paper No. 4 (London: Institute for Strategic Studies, May 1963), p. 12. Cf. Henry A. Kissinger, *The Troubled Partnership* (New York: McGraw-Hill, for the Council on Foreign Relations, 1965), p. 184.

[4] Kissinger, same, p. 19.

"excess deterrence," and one strategic concept (within the range of the current debate) may be as good as another. The present controversy may have as little objective basis as the debate over massive retaliation and forward strategy in the 1950s—or the disputations of the medieval schoolmen, which in abstractness and esoteric sophistication it sometimes resembles.

Yet whatever military historians may one day conclude about the objective merits of the strategic debate of the 1960s, it now divides the Alliance in a way which earlier controversies never did. There are two principal reasons why this is so. One is simply that in the 1960s disagreement does not jeopardize Europe's security and recovery as it would have in the 1950s, when the stability of the East-West confrontation was in doubt and Western Europe was still dependent on the United States for economic support. The European allies feel much freer to give a high priority to national concerns, including their views about strategy, and a correspondingly lower priority to agreement with the United States, than they did. Thus the "disarray" of the Alliance is in part the consequence of success.

But there is a more fundamental reason why controversy in the Alliance is more divisive today. In conditions of nuclear parity, the question of who controls the main deterrent becomes the central issue in the Atlantic relationship, and this issue is inherently divisive because it touches the most fundamental questions of national security and power.

Nuclear Control: The Issue

As long as America's nuclear monopoly or preponderance lasted, the question of nuclear control in the Alliance never really arose. Europeans could hardly doubt the credibility of the American nuclear threat. The stake of the United States in Europe's independence was great and obvious. Above all, the potential cost to the United States of fulfilling its guarantee was small. Although Europeans sometimes worried about whether the Soviets could be deterred by a nuclear threat alone, they did not question the determination of the President of the United States to pull the trigger if the Soviet Union attacked Western Europe. Thus they had little military reason to seek to share control of, or to find a means of triggering, the American deterrent. Moreover, as long as the Soviet Union lacked the capacity to damage the United States seriously, small British and French independent nuclear forces were not in any sense a threat to the security of the United States, since they could not provoke a Soviet nuclear attack against the United States.

Under conditions of nuclear parity, however, control of nuclear forces becomes the critical issue for all the major allies. In current American doctrine, American control of all the nuclear weapons of the Alliance (directly or by an American veto) is necessary to preserve centralized direction of escalation and to minimize the risk of general nuclear war. Central control is, indeed, essential if the decision when to initiate the use of nuclear weapons is to be made rapidly and rationally and in such a way as to minimize the probability of further escalation. Even if one remains unconvinced by the strategy which foresees a nicely controlled, graduated nuclear "bargaining" after nuclear hostilities have begun, nevertheless it is clear enough why the increase of Soviet strategic power has led the United States to assert its interest in unitary American control over the decision to begin using nuclear weapons.

American views on nuclear control also reflect more strictly political interests. When American spokesmen discount absolutely the utility of the French or British nuclear forces, or deny that there is any rational reason for Europeans to question the credibility of the American guarantee, or assert that there are no real differences in the strategic interests of Europeans and Americans, they are motivated (not always consciously) by a desire to preserve the nuclear basis of American leadership and prestige in the Alliance, and more particularly to maintain Germany's military dependence on the United States in order to reduce the possibility that Germany might one day seek to acquire nuclear weapons of her own.

French doctrine, in contrast, is more concerned with maximizing the deterrent threat and less with controlling escalation should deterrence fail. Further, it treats these two goals as separate and distinct and achievable by quite different means. For deterrence, the French stress the value of independent nuclear forces and a "multipolar" nuclear system. Since deterrence is the more effective, the more uncertain the enemy is about whether his action might provoke a nuclear response, it follows that several independent centers of nuclear control are more deterring than one, even though all but one are too small and too vulnerable to be by themselves an adequate deterrent.[5]

French strategic analysts recognize that the greater power of deterrence which a multipolar system creates is bought at the price of increasing the danger, in a crisis, that nuclear weapons would actually be used or that escalation would be uncontrolled. General André Beaufre and others have proposed that this danger be averted by providing for prearranged central direction of all the nuclear weapons of the Alliance in the event that a crisis occurs, or after war actually breaks out. They have suggested that the necessary coordination could be achieved by advance agreement among the allies on strategic doctrine and common plans.

Continuous consultation about strategy, and efforts to

[5] "The studies undertaken at the French Institute of Strategic Studies have shown that the deterrence of a potential adversary could be more complete if that adversary were faced with several centers of decision rather than only one. In this way the *multiplicity* of means, which tends to make a first strike more credible, is combined with *uncertainty*, mother of deterrence. The deterrent value of a multipolar system is therefore greater than of a system under unitary control." General André Beaufre, cited, p. 57.

reach agreement on doctrine and on contingency plans are surely desirable, if only because they acquaint the allies with each other's interests and attitudes and make coordination in a crisis that much easier. But the coordination achievable by this means should not be exaggerated. The allies are too far apart on strategy. Agreement, if reached, is apt to be in terms too general to control events; or if detailed plans are made they are likely to fit the actual shape of events only by a miracle. Consultation among allies cannot achieve the continuous, flexible coordination of action which is possible with unitary control. In practical effect, French doctrine so completely discounts the probability of war in Europe that the only consideration is deterrence, not control of escalation in a crisis or after hostilities have begun.

Indeed for France the motivation of nuclear policy seems to be primarily political. The *force de frappe* adds weight to President de Gaulle's assertion of national autonomy and to his claim to be leading Western Europe into independence from the "two foreign hegemonies." The government of France apparently believes that the American guarantee supplemented by the British and French nuclear forces is enough to deter the Soviet Union. Thus France is not concerned, as Germany is, either to make the American guarantee more automatic or to increase American involvement in Europe. That would be inconsistent with France's political objectives —in the short run, more French national autonomy; in the longer run more complete autonomy for a "Europe which is European."

Americans have been inclined to regard the strictly political and prestige aspects of small independent nuclear forces in Europe as unimportant or even as absurd and irrational, since they plainly do not give any European government an autonomous deterrent capability against the Soviet Union. But this is not the point. As Raymond Aron has said, Americans "are mistaken when they forget that possession of an atomic or thermonuclear force, even a minor one, can yield some authority within the framework of the Alliance, some prestige on the world scene, some diplomatic autonomy. The French are not alone in thinking that tomorrow there will be no great power without nuclear weapons, just as yesterday there was no great power without heavy industry and armored divisions. Even though this thermonuclear force is usable diplomatically neither against a great power nor against a small power, it fixes the status of states, their rank in the hierarchy of actors on the diplomatic-strategic stage." [6] When President de Gaulle or his minister of defense tells us that the nations of the world are divided into two categories, nuclear and non-nuclear, he is understating the difference in strictly military terms between the great nuclear power and the possessor of a small *force de frappe*. But he is not exaggerating the significance in terms of status and diplomatic influence which the possession of nuclear weapons yields.

German doctrine on nuclear control, although motivated by strategic considerations similar to those of the French, is far less radical in political terms. Its long Eastern frontier lacking natural defenses, its shape in an East-West direction lacking depth, West Germany, directly exposed to Soviet attack, is predisposed to a strategy of maximizing the deterrent threat. Still feeling too dependent on American good will to challenge United States' doctrine fundamentally, the Federal Republic seeks to assert its strategic interest in maximum deterrence within the framework of unitary American control.

Germany feels a deep sense of political and psychological dependence on the United States, and is anxious to consolidate the reconciliation with the West. Present German leaders themselves distrust German nationalism and fear the consequences of arousing their neighbors' distrust. All these factors predispose the Federal Republic to express its strategic interest by making the operation of the American nuclear guarantee

[6] Raymond Aron, *Paix et Guerre* (Paris: Calmann-Lévy, 1962), pp. 482–483.

as automatic as possible, rather than by seeking to supplement it with a national deterrent. Hence the German interest in tactical nuclear weapons under joint American-German control, and (at times) in proposals such as the Multilateral Force (MLF).

The British position on nuclear control, superficially similar to the French, is fundamentally quite different. The British independent nuclear program is older than the Atlantic Alliance itself. It was conceived when all of Europe was uncertain as to whether America's wartime commitment to European security would continue.[7] It antedates and thus is not a reaction to the notion that in the face of Soviet nuclear parity the American guarantee is unreliable. The British force has sometimes been officially justified in terms scarcely distinguishable from those which General de Gaulle has used about the *force de frappe*. But in practice British views on nuclear control today do not seem essentially inconsistent with American doctrine, whatever British ministers may say at election time about the value of an independent deterrent, because of the possibility that a future American administration might fail to maintain the guarantee. Basically, Britain still accepts willingly the leadership of the United States in the direction of NATO strategy. Her nuclear force is neither intended as a means of asserting an independent strategic doctrine nor of triggering a nuclear war which the United States is trying to avoid.

The United States feels it must, in its own vital interest, retain its control of the main deterrent, because the decision to use nuclear weapons has become a life-and-death matter for the United States. But for the European allies, the decision is also a matter of life and death. How, Europeans may well ask, can we be sure that the Americans will continue to value Europe's security as much as they do now? If we fail now to do something about sharing control of the American deterrent,

[7] Anthony Hartley, "The British Bomb." *Encounter,* May 1964, reprinted in *Survival,* July–August 1964, p. 172.

or about creating nuclear forces of our own, we shall be unprepared for that contingency (unlikely as it appears today), because it will be too late to remedy our neglect. The mounting of adequate European nuclear forces would take decades, not years. Thus many Europeans feel themselves driven by their security interests as well as by more strictly political concerns to seek to share control of the American deterrent, or, failing that, to build nuclear forces of their own.

To be sure, the issue today is not so sharp or so urgent as this summary statement might suggest, since on the whole Europeans now feel fairly secure about the deterrent effect of the American guarantee. But the issue is quite sharp enough to divide the allies seriously, and to make it probable that the questions of nuclear sharing and of the status of European nuclear forces will remain high on NATO's agenda for a long time to come.

Atlantic Nuclear Sharing

The term "nuclear sharing" covers a broad spectrum of ideas. Sometimes it means no more than sharing of American nuclear "secrets" and know-how, as the United States does with Britain under amendments to the MacMahon Act. Sometimes it means the participation by European military officers in American strategy making at the strictly technical level. This has been going on at SAC's Omaha headquarters since 1962. Sometimes it has referred to proposals like those which have been advanced from time to time for the addition to NATO's machinery of a new, high-level committee and staff for coordinating or planning the strategy, especially the nuclear strategy, of the Alliance; for example, the proposal made by Secretary of Defense McNamara in Paris on May 31, 1965, for a "select nuclear committee" of NATO defense ministers, [8] which was adopted in a modified form. Sometimes "sharing" refers to sharing control of a joint nuclear force

[8] *The New York Times,* June 1, 1965.

which is small relative to the American nuclear force, as in the American proposal for a Multilateral Force (MLF) and the British proposal for an Atlantic Nuclear Force (ANF).

We shall consider the significance of such arrangements presently. But first it is necessary to see what is involved if the term "nuclear sharing" is taken really seriously, as referring to an arrangement which shifts the locus of decision about strategy and the use of the main deterrent forces of the Alliance from the United States government to an allied council or agency. For it is only sharing in this radical sense which would meet the European desire for an effective voice in allied strategy making and in deciding when and how to use nuclear weapons.

A hypothetical example will serve to make the discussion a little clearer. The United States might place at the disposition of a NATO force enough of its Minuteman missiles and Polaris submarines to constitute, together with the French and British nuclear forces, a strategic nuclear force large enough to deter the Soviet Union. Tactical nuclear units in Europe might also be incorporated into the force. The Western nuclear powers, the United States, Britain, and France, would transfer nuclear forces to the joint force on the same basis; either all would be assigned on a long-term or "irrevocable" basis, or all would be merged into a jointly owned (and perhaps "mixed-manned") force. Non-nuclear powers wishing to participate could make financial contributions to a jointly owned component, which would make German participation possible without a national German nuclear contingent. Political control of the entire force, decisions about strategy, deployment, and use, would be in a board or council consisting of heads of governments or their deputies, deciding by unanimity. Thus the ultimate control would not be supranational, but by national agreement. The major contributors would each hold an effective veto in major decisions.

Such a force, if large and invulnerable enough, would

seem to be an adequate deterrent despite the absence of supranational authority. National vetoes would not necessarily impair fatally the credibility of the force as a deterrent, as long as its size and invulnerability were adequate in relation to the forces of the Soviet Union. One cannot presume a priori that British, French, and German vetoes would reduce the probability of an early use of nuclear weapons as compared with the present situation in which the United States is free to act; in some circumstances it might increase it, or appear to the Soviet Union to do so. The control board of a NATO force might well adopt a more "committal" strategic doctrine than the United States would adopt unilaterally.

Whether such a scheme would in fact shift the locus of nuclear control would depend on the size of the jointly controlled force relative to American nuclear forces remaining independent. If the remaining American force were large enough to be, in American eyes, an adequate deterrent to protect Europe, the scheme would involve no substantial change in the locus of control. For the United States could immobilize the joint force by interposing a veto, leaving itself free to determine unilaterally how and when its own force would be used. The joint force would, in these circumstances, remain dependent on American strategy and American decision. (This is one reason why European commentators were almost unanimous in pointing out that the American proposal for a Multilateral Force, however useful it might have been symbolically, to increase Europeans' sense of participation in nuclear defense, was not a scheme for nuclear sharing but rather a way of consolidating American control, "covering by artifice the unity of command which they [the Americans] wish to preserve.") [9] To give the principal European allies an effective voice in strategy making and nuclear control, it would be necessary to transfer enough of SAC's missiles and the navy's Polaris submarine fleet to an allied force to eliminate the uni-

[9] General André Beaufre, cited, p. 57.

lateral ability of the United States to make strategy for the Alliance and to determine how and when nuclear weapons would be used.

From an American standpoint, the difficulty of such a step is readily apparent. If the major part of the American military establishment were committed to an allied force, the United States would have committed itself to make foreign and military policy jointly with Western Europe—that is, to make its major policies for Europe and the rest of the world subject to British, French, and German vetoes. Could any president propose or any Congress accept so drastic and far-reaching a commitment of American power and limitation of American freedom of action?

Perhaps—but only if and only for so long as there existed a compelling military need to do so. Today and for the foreseeable tomorrow, however, there is no such military compulsion. Nor is it a sufficient inducement to the United States that many Europeans want nuclear sharing and that the American failure to respond divides the Alliance politically. For the European allies, because they have (for the time being, at least) no alternative to the Alliance, lack the ability to persuade or the power to demand so far-reaching a commitment of America's power to Europe's purposes.

Even were Western Europe to acquire, through a demonstrable will to unite and to provide for its own security, much more bargaining power, it cannot be presumed that the United States would prefer nuclear sharing to retaining its freedom of military and diplomatic action. Indeed, the latter might appear the more attractive of the two alternatives not only to the United States but to a united Western Europe as well. Why would Europeans make the immense effort required to unite, only to sacrifice their hard-won military and diplomatic autonomy by joining an Atlantic nuclear force?

The fundamental difficulty is that sharing control of the principal instruments of national power presupposes a deep consensus about the *purposes* for which military power can be used. These purposes are not limited to security. For a powerful nation or an ambitious one, military force is not a politically neutral instrument of security. It is also, and often primarily, a means to international status, an instrument for pursuing political objectives, a weapon to protect or propagate an ideology. Indeed, the political consensus which sharing of nuclear control would require is more than a particular convergence of national objectives. What genuine sharing would require is a common commitment by the allies to put the cohesion of the West, the Atlantic idea, ahead of all separate national interests—not just present interests but potential interests as well.

Such a commitment is characteristic of organized political communities. Its absence is equally characteristic of international relations. Genuine nuclear sharing would be possible only if the principal allies were determined to make of their association something much more than an alliance: namely, an organized political community. The dilemmas of strategy and nuclear control in the Alliance could be resolved only if the Alliance were ready to move toward some form of Atlantic political union.

In the long history of alliances, the problem of joint control of forces has usually proved insoluble. Even when the military situation cries out for truly joint control of allied forces, the political prerequisites are usually lacking, especially in time of peace. In wartime, the necessary identity of political and strategic aims has at times been produced temporarily by the exigencies of the military situation, although even then the requisite unity of purpose is seldom achieved unless one ally is much more powerful than the others, as in the Anglo-American alliance in World War II and the Rome-Berlin Axis. In peacetime the military need is less compelling, and the allies' political and strategic interests tend to diverge. Joint control in a substantial sense becomes impossible, unless the alliance is much more than an alliance—namely, an incipient political community. Only when political unity as an end in itself becomes an overriding objective can the necessary convergence of particular political and strategic interests be achieved. This is why genuine Atlantic nuclear sharing—joint control of the principal nuclear forces of the Alliance—is now impossible.

The MLF Story

If this conclusion is correct, it goes a long way to explain the trials and tribulations of the principal attempt so far made to come to grips with the problem of nuclear sharing in the Alliance, the American proposal for a Multilateral Force or MLF. The MLF, to recall briefly its principal features, was to have consisted of some twenty-five missile-carrying surface vessels, each armed with eight Polaris nuclear missiles, capable of reaching, from the ships' anticipated stations, any target in the Soviet Union. Although the official military mission of the force was to balance the large Soviet preponderance of medium-range ballistic missiles targeted on Western Europe, the force would also have been an addition to the general strategic nuclear capability of the Alliance, although a small one compared with the American strategic force.

The force was to have consisted, not of assigned national contingents, but of vessels, weapons, and facilities jointly owned by the participating governments and manned by crews of mixed nationality ("mixed-manned") subject to a denationalized operational command. All major decisions were to have been made by an executive committee representing the principal contributing countries. Voting rights in this committee were to have reflected financial contributions, which were to have been so ordered that the United States, Britain, and Germany (and France if she were ever to join) would each have had a veto. Thus basic decisions about strategy and the use of the force would have been by unanimity of the principal members. To prevent France from blocking the proposal, the force was not to have been formally part of NATO. It would, nevertheless, have become the most significant institution of the Alliance.[10]

American spokesmen presented the MLF as a step toward meeting European desires for sharing nuclear control. But if the preceding analysis of nuclear sharing is correct, an arrangement such as MLF would not involve sharing in a genuine sense because it would not alter materially the locus of power. No doubt the European governments would have been in a somewhat better position to influence American strategy by reason of their participation in MLF, in part because their competence in nuclear weaponry and strategy would have increased, in part because their agreement would have been required to coordinate the MLF with American forces. But the power to decide when and where to use nuclear weapons would remain in the American president and in him alone— not essentially because of the American veto but because of the size of the MLF as compared with American nuclear forces.[11] The United States alone would have been capable of making an independent nuclear decision, even after an MLF had been established. MLF would have remained a supplement to the American forces, unable to act independently. The MLF proposal involved nuclear sharing in a symbolic and psychological sense, but not the sharing of nuclear control.

We do not, however, suggest that American officials and commentators were disingenuous about MLF, or that they were mistaken in urging the proposal upon the European governments. The policy was sound from the standpoint of Amer-

---

[10] The most explicit official American public statement of the MLF proposal is contained in an address by Gerard C. Smith, Special Adviser to the Secretary of State, entitled "The Nuclear Defense of NATO," delivered at Annapolis, Maryland on April 22, 1964, *Department of State Press Release* No. 178.

[11] Cf. Robert E. Osgood, *The Case for the MLF: A Critical Evaluation* (The Washington Center of Foreign Policy Research, 1964), pp. 19–20.

ican strategic and political interests: the prevention of the spread of nuclear weapons to Germany; the maintenance of the American nuclear protectorate of Europe; the integration of Germany's military contribution to the Alliance under allied (essentially American) control. We have seen that the integration of Germany's conventional forces under SHAPE's command serves American interests on a basis acceptable to Germans and many other Europeans. The MLF proposal was an attempt to apply the same principle to strategic nuclear weapons. In the circumstances, the United States naturally attempted to make the form of sharing (a small, jointly controlled force) substitute for its reality (a seat on the control board of the real deterrent). The MLF made sense in terms of American interests precisely because it was *not* a step toward the sharing of nuclear control, but rather a way of channeling Europe's—especially Germany's—nuclear interests and energies away from the development of independent nuclear forces.

That this was the real basis of American policy on MLF, whatever promises spokesmen may have held out about nuclear sharing, is strongly suggested by the fact that vigorous American support of the proposal came only gradually and as a direct response to the unfolding of President de Gaulle's European objectives, and to a growing fear of their effect on Germany. It was not until the political meaning of De Gaulle's veto in January 1963 of British entry into the Common Market had been grasped in the United States that the administration, although still hesitantly, began to throw its full diplomatic weight behind MLF. The change of emphasis and pace seems to have been intended essentially to avert a possible Franco-German military collaboration, with the implicit danger that it would lead to some kind of independent German nuclear deterrent, or to German participation in a Franco-German nuclear force.

We shall not enter the lists on the issue of whether or not

the MLF proposal whetted a German nuclear appetite which did not previously exist. The problem of Germany's nuclear future is not firmly on the Atlantic agenda. As China's nuclear power grows, as India and other countries contemplate nuclear weapons, the question of a German force is likely to become more pressing. The Federal Republic will be increasingly tempted to heed the lesson of General de Gaulle, take the solidity of the American guarantee for granted, and pursue a more autonomous foreign policy, in order to increase bargaining power with the United States and the Soviet Union on reunification. Were this to happen, some Germans might conclude that a nuclear force of their own, or a threat to acquire it, would be a useful bargaining counter in dealing with the East. So far these somber possibilities lie in the future. Fortunately, the Federal Republic is still too firmly attached to the United States, too concerned for its security and, indeed, fearful of itself. Scarcely a voice can be heard in Germany for an independent national nuclear role. Yet it would be ungenerous to fault American officials for trying to avert that possibility.[12]

The MLF would also have discouraged the emergence of a *collective* European nuclear force by tending to perpetuate the organization of the Western defenses on an Atlantic basis and by placing a new institutional and financial obstacle in the way. Official American statements often presented the proposal as including the possibility that a European nuclear force of some kind could eventually develop out of the MLF. This was to be achieved by the relinquishing of the American veto, or, more radically, by separating off a European force. But such statements, however intended, seem in reality to have meant little more than the rather remote prognostication

[12] The Federal Republic, in the treaties by which it gained its sovereignty in 1954, renounced production of nuclear weapons on German territory. It did not, however, give up the right to own them, much less the right to participate in a joint arrangement for production and control of nuclear weapons with France or any other power.

that when and if Europe should achieve political unity, a new situation would have been created which would affect the whole structure of the Alliance, including an MLF if one were then in existence. Verbal support for a remote "European nuclear option" was not necessarily inconsistent with a proposal whose practical effect would be to place an obstacle in the way of a collective European nuclear force.

In Europe the MLF proposal was positively supported, for its own sake, only by Chancellor Erhard's government in Germany. German support was not based on the belief that the MLF held out the promise of real participation in control of the main deterrent, but rather on the assumption that it would be a new link in the American nuclear guarantee.[13] The fact that the political aim of the proposal was to put an obstacle in the way of any future German nuclear ambitions was not at the time a serious objection in Germany, for most Germans were nearly as anxious as Americans to foreclose the possibility of an independent German nuclear force.

In Britain, both the Macmillan government (before the 1964 election) and the Wilson government were cool to the MLF. Labour's opposition stemmed in part from the pacifist and anti-German tradition of Labour's Left Wing, and also from a fear that the MLF might endanger the possibility of agreement with the Soviet Union on arms control and disarmament. Also weighty in Labour's councils was the financial burden which MLF in its original form would have imposed on a seriously overstrained British economy and balance of payments.

[13] As Fritz Erler, foreign-policy spokesman for the German Socialist party, put it, "Only genuine integration, which means the merging of definite units in peacetime and the creation of common command structures and common planning, can assure an automatic military answer to an action of a conceivable opponent. . . . The MLF, which goes beyond the current treaty text by committing definite portions of the American atomic potential to permanent involvement with European forces, represents an especially valuable reinforcement of the American engagement in Europe and thus of the general credibility of the deterrent." Paper dated October 13, 1964, prepared for meeting of the *Atlantik-Brücke* and the American Council on Germany, Berlin, November 12–15, 1964 (mimeographed), p. 7.

Nevertheless, many in Britain have recognized that if some new Atlantic nuclear arrangement were to be made, the British would have to join, if only to prevent its becoming a bilateral German-American affair. A German-American "special relationship" in nuclear matters could only have the effect of enhancing German influence in Europe at Britain's expense. Moreover, Harold Wilson had made a campaign promise to get rid of Britain's independent nuclear forces. Both purposes might have been achieved, without an additional burden on the overloaded Exchequer, if the British nuclear forces could be transferred to a new Atlantic nuclear force, in which Britain, by reason of this large contribution, would have a voice at least equal to Germany's. Reasoning of this kind seems to have been behind the decision of the Wilson government in late 1964 to support, not the original MLF, but an Atlantic nuclear force (ANF) in which there would be a small mixed-manned element to allow for German participation on a non-national basis, together with a larger force made up of national contingents—British, American, and hopefully one day French as well—assigned to the Atlantic force "for as long as the Alliance lasts," as Wilson put it in the House of Commons on December 16, 1964. According to the British plan, the political control of the force would have been by the unanimous decision of the major participants.

Thus in late 1964 the Wilson government seemed to be moving away from nuclear independence and toward a more consistently "Atlantic" approach to the issue of nuclear control. The British recognize that the cost of keeping up with the superpowers in military technology, which already exceeds Britain's capabilities, is growing. But political objectives parallel to those of the United States were probably the main motive. Gaullist sentiment on the Continent raised for Britain as for the United States the unwelcome prospect of a nuclear "Europe" excluding Britain, built around a Franco-German coalition—or, worse, a nuclear Germany bent on pursuing independently its Eastern interests. A new Atlantic nuclear arrangement which included Germany on a thoroughly integrated basis could perhaps forestall such an outcome.

So matters stood in December 1964. It then appeared that with continued American pressure, particularly on Bonn, agreement would be reached on some kind of Atlantic nuclear force to include Britain, Germany, Italy, and the Netherlands over the determined opposition of France.

Yet at this point the evolution was dramatically interrupted when the United States administration, success seemingly within its grasp, backed away. Serious opposition had developed within the administration and Congress to forcing through a proposal which only Germany really supported (and not wholeheartedly), which De Gaulle strongly opposed, and which had little positive support in the rest of NATO Europe. The President issued a blunt memorandum to the executive agencies through the National Security Council whose meaning was clear: there would be no MLF or ANF unless and until the British and the Germans had agreed, without American pressure, on its terms.[14] In effect, the administration acted as if MLF or ANF were a concession which the United States was offering Europe, although the American interest in the proposals was at least as great as Britain's or Germany's, and the obligation of leadership was America's not Europe's.

Thus at the critical moment American leadership was withdrawn, and De Gaulle was allowed to win by default his battle against strengthening the Atlantic nuclear tie, without even having to exert real pressure on the Germans. It was unfortunate. As events were soon to prove, the opportunity to tie Germany more closely into the Alliance and put an obstacle in the way of German and European nuclear independence which was missed in 1964 may not come soon again.

A hiatus of nearly a year ensued, while America and Europe awaited the outcome of the German elections of Septem-

[14] *The New York Times*, December 22, 1964.

ber 1965. During that year a new issue was injected into the nuclear control debate which, in the end, sealed the fate of MLF and ANF. The United Nations Disarmament Committee, which had been dormant for several years, suddenly came to life when the Soviet Union evinced an unexpected interest in a proposal for a treaty to prohibit the "dissemination" of nuclear weapons by any nuclear power to any non-nuclear power.

The Russian motive was not obscure; it was to prevent Germany from acquiring control of nuclear weapons or taking any steps which might lead in that direction. Wisely from their standpoint, the Russians did not waste much time denouncing Germany's existing access to tactical nuclear weapons under the "two-key" or "double-veto" system. Instead, they directed their fire at the MLF-ANF issue and sought to have included in the treaty a provision which would prohibit the turning over of nuclear weapons to any such joint force, even though the United States retained a veto over their use.

The Western powers rejected the Soviet proposal, maintaining that the transfer of nuclear weapons to an allied force in which the United States and Britain retain vetoes should not be considered dissemination within the meaning of the proposed treaty. Nevertheless, Soviet diplomacy was successful in dividing Western opinion on MLF still further. Many Americans and Britons saw the anti-dissemination treaty as an important new step toward world peace and joined the opposition to an Atlantic nuclear force, on the ground that it was the only remaining obstacle to agreement with the Soviet Union.

Those who reasoned thus apparently felt that an agreement with the Soviet Union prohibiting the Russians from doing something which they had no apparent intention or interest in doing (giving nuclear weapons to a non-nuclear country) was worth the price of tying Western hands in a matter of the most vital Western interest: nuclear arrangements within the Atlantic Alliance. They were willing to abandon one of the wisest tenets of American and British postwar policy—that the best and safest international role for Germany is one in which she participates as an equal in integrated institutional arrangements, Atlantic and European—in favor of the dubious notion that the way to control Germany is by an American-Russian entente.

Even in Germany the Soviet maneuver was successful. The Socialists, who had supported the MLF in 1964 on the ground that it would strengthen the American commitment to Germany's security and reduce Gaullist influence in Europe, withdrew their support. Their reason was apparently a growing belief that the prospects of German reunification would be seriously compromised if Germany participated in a new Atlantic nuclear force over the strenuous objections of her Eastern neighbors and the Soviet Union.

Meanwhile, the opposition to MLF within Chancellor Erhard's own party and from Franz Josef Strauss's Christian Social Union had also increased. This opposition was based in part on a reluctance to part company with De Gaulle and in part on a disinclination to place any obstacle in the way of the eventual emergence of a European nuclear force independent of the United States—a force whose basis would be Franco-German nuclear collaboration. As Strauss put it in an article published in April 1965, "But how can one imagine a political union in Western Europe with no freedom of decision in questions of defence? Yet that is precisely what would have been the inevitable result if the MLF had come into existence. The Europe called for by President Kennedy. . . . A Europe which, speaking with *one* voice, was to become a genuine and valuable partner of America, could never become a reality if it lacked so significant an element of sovereign policy." [15]

In this way the tenuous American-British-German consensus which had existed in December 1964, on which it

[15] "An Alliance of Continents," *International Affairs*, April 1965, p. 199. See also *The New York Times*, October 30, 1965.

would probably have been possible to erect an integrated Atlantic nuclear force of some kind, unraveled. A year later, on December 21, 1965, President Johnson and Chancellor Erhard, on the occasion of the German leader's visit to Washington, buried the MLF in silence, promising each other only that the issue of nuclear control would not be forgotten.[16]

The lesson to be drawn from this frustrating story is that there is no solution to the problem of nuclear control which satisfies the needs and interests of all the major allies. The United States is not able to offer its European allies a real share in control of the principal nuclear forces of the Alliance, although that is the only offer which would fully meet the European allies' legitimate desire to share in the decisions about the use of the awful weapons on which their very existence depends. The United States is unable to do this, not because many Americans would not like to if they could, but because the political prerequisites are lacking—because the joint management of the major military forces of the Alliance presupposes an Atlantic political community which does not exist.

Because the United States is not able to offer Europeans what they really want, the United States cannot obtain major concessions from the European allies on the nuclear issues in which the United States is primarily interested. It cannot, for example, expect the French, or even the British, to give up their independent nuclear forces. It cannot expect that those Europeans who look forward to a united Europe able to provide for its own security will give up that hope in exchange for some largely symbolic sharing (as in MLF) or for a new NATO committee to talk about nuclear matters.

But the fact that the nuclear control problem cannot be resolved to the complete satisfaction of the principal parties at interest is not a sufficient reason for the United States to stop trying to find a substitute that is satisfactory in part. Above all,

16 *The New York Times,* December 22, 1965.

it is not a reason for Americans to lose sight of their real interests in the nuclear problem, which center on the question of how to give West Germany a worthy, constructive, and nonnationalistic role in nuclear deterrence.

The answer will not be found in a United States–Soviet understanding that Germany should never be allowed access to nuclear weapons. A policy of this kind would defeat itself. It would alienate German opinion. Its final result would be to persuade Germans that they have no alternative to looking out for their own interests in nuclear matters, which is precisely what the United States should seek to avoid. The problem is to find a way to enlist Germany in the cause of integrated Atlantic nuclear arrangements which make it possible for Germans to play a larger part in the maintenance of the nuclear balance of power on which their security depends.

At this moment, when the first serious attempt to find a means to this end has just failed and no feasible alternative is in sight, it is difficult for the United States to act. For the time being, therefore, it is best to wait. Indeed, the United States has no other option, as long as Germans are as divided as they are on nuclear control. At a later time perhaps it will be possible to revive the idea of an integrated multilateral Atlantic force.

Sooner or later the question of a European collective nuclear force not subject to an American veto will arise; so far it has not been an actual issue but only a potential one. A European nuclear force, conceived in a separatist Gaullist spirit, would be contrary to American interests. But conceived in a different spirit, and with British participation, it might prove a tolerable substitute for an integrated Atlantic nuclear force, and thus a way of meeting Germany's desire to participate in nuclear strategy making and control on a basis acceptable to her allies. We return to this question in Chapter 5.

CHAPTER THREE

Control of
International Money

The economies of the Atlantic nations are rather highly integrated. This means that formal barriers to trade (at least in manufactured products) and to international payments are relatively low. It also means that the extent to which these economies interpenetrate is relatively high; their domestic economic balance and their international payments react rather sensitively to changes in prices, costs and monetary conditions in each others' economies. These things are true, at any rate, in comparison with any previous historical period. The economic integration of the Atlantic Community is unprecedented both in degree and in kind.

The pre-1914 trading world of Europe, the United States, and the colonial empires was integrated also, in the sense that public barriers to trade and payments were not very restrictive, and that general political conditions were favorable to international trade and investment. But the degree of integration in a more strictly economic sense was a great deal less than it is now. Real transport costs were much higher, and national economies were much less integrated internally. The stage of industrial development was such that the trading countries did not penetrate each others' markets to anything like the extent they do today.

The difference between integration before 1914 and Atlantic economic integration today is as much qualitative as quantitative. Before 1914 governments were little involved in management and control of the economy. They were not held responsible for employment, growth, price stability, and the other aspects of economic welfare which are the principal domestic business of government in the mid-twentieth century. In our times, therefore, the maintenance of a high degree of international economic integration presupposes an unprecedented capacity for cooperation or parallel action by national economic authorities. Without it, conflict or inconsistency among national economic policies would make it necessary for governments to restrict trade and payments—that is, to reduce international integration—in order to be able to fulfill their domestic responsibilities.

The problem of reconciling national economic objectives with international economic integration comes to a head in the balance of international payments. Or, as it is usually put, the state of a country's balance of payments, particularly if its payments are seriously in deficit and means of financing are not ample, exercises a serious constraint on its freedom in respect of employment, growth, and price policy, as long as the government desires to avoid imposing major new restrictions on its external payments. These domestic objectives touch nearly every citizen's pocketbook. Thus for a group of economies as integrated as those of the Atlantic Community, the problem of monetary autonomy and international integration is inevitably an important and a difficult one.

In this chapter we explore this problem in the form in which it presents itself today: the problem of the United States' balance of payments and the question of reform of the international monetary system. As we shall see, the problem parallels in many ways the controversy about military strategy and control of nuclear weapons in the Alliance. It is a controversy between the United States and the principal countries of continental Europe over the objectives of the international monetary system and over the question of who is to control the process of reserve-creation.

The stress, then, will be on differences. But it should not be overlooked that the differences take the form they do because the Atlantic economy is so integrated and because the Atlantic governments have a common interest in keeping it that way. As in Atlantic military, so in Atlantic monetary matters: the conflict takes place within a framework of interdependence whose continuation is taken for granted.

Before we turn to the specifics of the Atlantic monetary issue, a little background on the present international monetary system and its antecedents may be useful.

The Present System and Its Antecedents

The gold standard is long gone, but it remains a fertile source of insight into the problems of international monetary order. Unfortunately for our purposes, the usual descriptions of the gold standard focus attention on its mechanics and take for granted the institutional framework and the political conditions which made the mechanism possible. The system is described as one in which the participating countries' common concern was to maintain stable gold parities for their currencies. Given this overriding concern, and in view of the fact that gold had come to be the only regular means of international settlement and the principal element in bank reserves, the conditions of credit in all countries were geared directly to the state of the balance of payments. Thus freedom of trade and payments and stability of parities were maintained automatically.

The emphasis on the function of gold movements before 1914 tends to obscure the fact that the system was a sterling system whose functioning depended as much on the central control over credit exercised by the City of London as on the mechanics of gold. Sterling was the medium in which nearly all international business was done (the "vehicle currency" of the day, as Robert Roosa called it), while the credit operations of the City were the principal means of financing balance-of-payments deficits. Because Britain was the only large exporter of capital and because there were no important competing financial centers, these credit operations exerted a central and frequently determining influence on monetary conditions and the state of the balance of payments throughout the trading world.[1]

The traditional account of the gold standard describes the role of the Bank of England and the London money market as a passive, automatic response to market forces and gold movements. The institutions of the City were indeed nonpolitical; they worked for private profit, not for public purposes. They functioned, nevertheless, with a degree of discretion which we must recognize as evidence of immense financial power. It is improbable that the system would have worked well or lasted long without this central control.[2] Today General de Gaulle

[1] "Because exchange rates were stable in terms of each other, national money markets came to be linked by an effective system of international short- and long-term credit, centered primarily in London. These links permitted changes in the volume and direction of credit flows, rather than flows of gold, to keep international accounts in balance. . . . British financial dominance was essential for the adjustment mechanism that operated in the nineteenth century." Hans O. Schmitt, "Political Conditions for International Currency Reform" (Reprint No. 81, Social Systems Research Institute, Madison, Wisconsin, 1964), quoted in Robert A. Mundell, *The International Monetary System: Conflict and Reform* (Montreal: Canadian Trade Committee of the Private Planning Association of Canada, 1965), p. 22.

[2] "The Bank of England, the London money market, the sterling-gold standard system—and the anonymous authorities in London who managed them—were essential to the maintenance of a unified monetary system covering the entire trading world. The habit of regarding these institutions and mechanisms as wholly automatic and impersonal—even as 'natural'—was a tribute to their extraordinary effectiveness before World War I and was, indeed, one of the reasons for their effectiveness. But this habit has obscured the fact that one of the major elements in the successful operation of the sterling-gold standard system was the possession of great discretionary power by a small number of men in London and the absence of

invokes the gold standard in the cause of French autonomy, but the historical gold standard was run from London.

Moreover, the gold standard presupposed that participating governments would generally put freedom of payments and stability of parities ahead of any other economic consideration, at least in time of peace. This commitment was taken for granted. It was not so much a deliberate choice as an ideological position, the adherence as a matter of principle to economic liberalism and *laissez faire*. Thus the City was free to exercise its controlling influence, and the governments of other countries did not presume to interfere with the customary responses of their bankers to gold losses or gains, regardless of the effect on prices, production, or employment.

The breakdown of the gold-standard system can be explained by the erosion of these essential conditions of its functioning. As long as governments allowed monetary policy to be made for all in London and put stability of parities and international financial integration ahead of other economic objectives, the gold standard worked well. It ceased to do so after World War I, because these conditions no longer obtained. Partially reconstituted after 1918, although with important modifications,[3] it broke down completely in the 1930s, having first played a large part in intensifying and spreading the collapse of credit which initiated general deflation. In the circumstances, governments had to assume re-

---

other important competing financial centers." W. Y. Elliot, H. van B. Cleveland, Theodore Geiger, and others, *The Political Economy of American Foreign Policy* (New York: Henry Holt, 1955), p. 26.

[3] The modification most relevant to this inquiry was the practice of European central banks after 1918 of supplementing their gold reserves by holding sterling and to a lesser extent dollars as reserve assets. Existing reserves had become grossly inadequate, especially in continental Europe, because of Europe's extraordinary import requirements for reconstruction, and because sterling and the dollar remained at their 1914 gold parities (until 1931 and 1933, respectively), although the prices of British and American exports had greatly increased. The practice of holding sterling and dollars along with gold as reserve assets was formalized at an international monetary conference in 1922. It changed the gold standard into a gold-exchange standard and laid the technical basis for the gold-dollar system which prevails today.

sponsibility for raising domestic demand and employment. To do so they found they had to nationalize monetary policy—to sever the direct link between domestic credit, gold, and the balance of payments and to assert political control over central banks and banking systems. In an effort to increase production and exports, governments resorted to high tariffs, import quotas, competitive devaluation, and other beggar-thy-neighbor policies which soon destroyed what remained of the integration which had characterized the trading world before 1914. The international monetary system was reduced to a shadow of the old system. What remained was little more than a means of clearing and settling artificially controlled balances among increasingly isolated national monetary systems, in which domestic employment had come to have a nearly absolute priority over international integration.

When the delegates of the Atlantic nations met at Bretton Woods to write the rules of an international monetary system for the postwar world, the monetary traumas of the 1930s were uppermost in their minds. The delegates were preoccupied with the fear of a postwar depression and with a desire to prevent a recurrence of the 1930s. They sought to preserve to the members sufficient autonomy of monetary and fiscal policy to make effective employment policies possible, without authorizing competitive devaluations and preventing a reasonable degree of freedom of trade and payments.

The system devised to accomplish this difficult balance was set forth in the Articles of Agreement of the International Monetary Fund (IMF). After a transition period, members were required to make their currencies freely convertible with one another for transactions on current account, but not for capital transactions. It was assumed that members would normally use exchange control on capital movements for balance-of-payments purposes—in particular, to prevent speculative capital movements and capital flight of the kind which had contributed to the downfall of the gold standard. Thus a member country was to be relatively free to pursue a credit policy appropriate to its domestic needs, without undue concern for the effect of international differences in interest rates on capital movements and the balance of payments. Markets for goods and services were to be integrated internationally, but not markets for capital and money.

The Agreement contemplated that imbalances of payments were to be corrected, not in the main by internal adjustments of prices, demand, and employment as under the gold standard, but by adjusting exchange rates. To inhibit disorderly competitive devaluation, members were required to file official rates with the Fund, which could be changed only in cases where "fundamental" imbalance was found by the executive board of the Fund. The Agreement contemplated neither the stability of parities nor the integration of capital markets which the gold standard involved. Their sacrifice was thought a reasonable price to pay for greater autonomy of national economic policy.

Nor did the Bretton Woods Agreement contemplate the need for any central control of credit nor for a large new source of international credit. Lord Keynes, who headed the British delegation at Bretton Woods, had earlier proposed an ambitious plan for a world monetary authority (which he euphemistically called a clearing union) with extensive supranational credit powers and authority to condition the granting of credit on changes in exchange rates and to recommend changes in domestic policies. But the United States opposed it in favor of the much more modest IMF, and the American view prevailed. The Agreement gave each member a right to draw currencies of other members from the Fund within the limits of an assigned quota, a part of which was available on demand and a part at the discretion of the executive board. But the quotas were not large; the Fund's credit operations were intended to help temporarily to finance relatively small deficits, pending a decision whether the deficits were sufficiently "fundamental" to require an adjustment of rates. It was assumed, in other words, that international payments would not remain out of balance long, because deficits and surpluses would be dealt with quickly and decisively, by devaluation if necessary. Thus central control of the creation and distribution of international reserves or credit was not considered a major issue, let alone a function without which an international monetary system could not work well.

The delegates at Bretton Woods sought to establish a system fundamentally different from the sterling-gold standard system. Yet the new system that grew up within the general framework of the Charter turned out to be surprisingly like the old one. In the first place, the postwar system came to depend on the central function of the banking and financial authorities of the United States, which assumed the former role of the City of London as the principal source of international capital and the regulator of international liquidity and monetary conditions. The dominant role of the United States in the system was not, to be sure, the deliberate result of American policy or ambition. Like nuclear preponderance, it was the unintended consequence of World War II, which so greatly enhanced America's economic power, while European power was in eclipse. Because the American economy is so large, because prices here have been relatively stable, because foreign aid and military dollars by the tens of billions were poured into Europe, because the United States is the only major international source of investment capital and short-term funds, because the American capital and money markets are so large and efficient, and because the supply of monetary gold was growing much more slowly than the world's need for reserves, it was well-nigh inevitable that the dollar would become the principal vehicle currency and reserve asset for most of the non-Communist world. Consequently, American domestic monetary conditions, and the policies of the Federal Reserve Board in Washington, came to have a controlling influence on international liquidity and, therefore, a large impact on domestic monetary conditions in other countries.

The existing monetary system differs fundamentally from the Bretton Woods blueprint in other respects as well. Instead of the "adjustable peg" arrangement intended by the Charter, in which exchange rates would be changed to correct "fundamental" payments imbalances, the present system involves a strong presumption in favor of stable rates of exchange. In part this has been owing to the natural bias of international bankers, traders, and investors toward stability in the value of the currencies in which their calculations are made. Governments, for their part, resist rate changes, because they wish to discourage speculation; because they fear that the competitive advantage of any devaluation would be offset by other devaluations, at least in the case of a major currency; and because in the case of dollars and sterling the United States and Britain anticipate (no doubt correctly) that confidence in their value as reserve assets would be shaken. Governments and central banks which are poles apart on the issue of international monetary reform have nevertheless been able to agree on support measures when the pound, the lira, or the dollar has been under heavy speculative pressure. Indeed, stability of parities seems to have become very nearly the article of faith it was under the gold standard.[4]

Stable parities encourage trade and investment and make for greater international economic integration. Similarly, the fact that the large and efficient American capital and money markets have been, until recently, freely open to all comers has linked the money markets of the Atlantic nations, even though most other countries restrict access by foreigners to their financial markets. In consequence, movements of short-term funds into and out of the United States have been sensitive

[4] As noted in Chapter 5, page 133, the decision to fix common agricultural prices within the European Economic Community tends to fix the parity of the six members' currencies relative to each other, adding a further bias toward rate stability in the international monetary system.

to international differences in interest rates, and to speculative influences, quite contrary to plan.

These departures from Bretton Woods served well the common interest of the Atlantic nations in a more efficient, integrated international economy, but they created a monetary system which is inherently problematic. On the one hand, the principal means of redressing payments imbalances foreseen by the IMF Agreement (rate adjustments and exchange controls on capital account) were eliminated. On the other hand, the willingness of governments to subordinate national economic objectives to the discipline of the balance of payments has not increased sufficiently to compensate. The Atlantic governments have generally tried, to the extent their reserves or access to international credits have permitted, to give priority to national objectives.

Nevertheless, the system worked and worked well as long as there was an ample source of international liquidity or credit to finance imbalances until they could be corrected. It worked, that is, as long as the United States was allowed to function as central banker (and therefore controller) of the system: as long as other governments were willing, or felt compelled, to rely on the United States to supply (through aid and military spending and the export of capital) the funds which made it possible for all, including the United States, to finance imbalances. That essential condition has now ceased in part to exist. Just as the gold standard was undermined when the anonymous monetary authorities in London were dethroned, so the present system is threatened by the growing resistance of continental Europe to the dominant role of the dollar.

In sum, an international monetary system in which exchange rate changes are largely ruled out, in which governments would prefer to give national objectives a higher priority than balance in the external accounts, and in which capital and money markets are linked across national frontiers, will not work well unless there is a large source of acceptable international money (liquidity) or credit readily accessible to countries which run into balance-of-payments difficulties. "A fixed rate system, if it is to permit correction of payments disequilibria in a manner consistent with other policy objectives, must be able to tolerate slow corrections. This means it must be able to provide financing for substantial and protracted deficits of the major industrial countries." [5] If the United States is no longer able to provide financing unilaterally, it remains to be seen whether any substitute by way of international cooperation can be found. But before we consider the question of international monetary reform we must look more closely into the reasons why the United States is no longer able to play its former monetary role.

The Parties and the Issue

The Atlantic monetary issue parallels the nuclear issue. It is a controversy between the United States and the members of the European Economic Community about strategy and control. The question of strategy concerns the significance of and the responsibility for the deficit in the United States balance of payments. Should the deficit be corrected promptly by internal measures or by controls, or should it be financed until it gradually corrects itself? If it should be corrected promptly, who has the principal responsibility, Europe or America? The control issue is about who decides whether this and other deficits are to be financed or corrected and to what extent. Who is to control the expansion and contraction of international reserves (liquidity) generally?

The principal parties to the monetary issue, then, are the United States and the members of the Common Market. The alignment reflects the structure of international payments rela-

<hr>

[5] Walter Salant, *Does the International Monetary System Need Reform?* (Washington: The Brookings Institution, 1964), p. 16.

tions. Since 1950 the United States' balance of payments has been in deficit in every year but one. The counterpart of this deficit has been a surplus concentrated in continental Europe, particularly the Europe of the Six, whose reserves of gold and dollars in consequence increased in this period (1950–62) by some $17 billion.[6] Most other countries, Britain included, have been on the average, in balance, spending currently as much foreign exchange as they earn but no more. Their demand for imports has been too insistent, or their competitive position too weak, to permit accumulating reserves; their reserves have been too slim to finance persistent deficits.

The dollar deficit, then, is primarily a United States–EEC affair. Other countries are interested—vitally interested—but less directly responsible and with far less influence on the outcome. Even Britain is unable to play the role to which her size, traditions, and the reserve status of sterling would otherwise entitle her, due to chronic financial weakness.

The dollar deficit is not itself the issue, however. The deficit ran for more than a decade without becoming a source of trans-Atlantic controversy. Throughout the 1950s it was simply the unintended and uncontroversial reflection of American foreign aid and military expenditures, and of the normal operations of an international monetary system in which the currency of the leading country is used by traders for their working balances and by central banks to supplement gold reserves. It was not the result of decisions by European governments to finance it, or of a decision by the United States government to seek such financing. European central banks accumulated dollar balances, not because they wished to extend credit to the United States, but because they desired to

---

[6] Walter Salant and Emile Despres, *The United States Balance of Payments in 1968* (Washington: The Brookings Institution, 1963), pp. 23–30. Other continental European countries' gold and dollar reserves increased by about $5 billion in the same period, while British reserves declined. Canadian reserves have been more or less level over the period. Japan's reserves rose until 1960 and have been level or slightly falling since.

replenish reserves depleted by war and reconstruction, in the form of interest-bearing claims rather than in gold. They did so the more willingly, because the claims were on the largest and most advanced economy in the world, the economy with the best record of price and exchange stability over the years, and with the largest gold reserve.

Indeed until 1960, when this happy congruence of European and American interests began to break down, it could be argued that there was no deficit, if "deficit" means an imbalance in need of rapid correction. As long as European central banks willingly accumulated dollars which were surplus to the current needs of European traders, the deficit was, at it were, self-financing.

Dollars received by Europeans in excess of current needs are normally purchased by the central bank, in exchange for local currency, in the course of its exchange stabilization operations. Under IMF rules, member governments are required to keep their exchange rates within 1 per cent of the official rate on file with the Fund. This is normally accomplished by purchases and sales of dollars for local currency by the central bank. Thus dollars in Europe surplus to current business needs find their way into the hands of the central bank. Otherwise the surplus would tend to drive the European currency's rate up beyond the 1 per cent limit. The accumulation of dollars by the European central banks amounted to an extension of credit to the United States.

European objections to a dollar deficit are a compound of financial, economic, and political considerations. Central bankers and finance ministers are uneasy about accumulating dollars in excess of foreseeable needs. It is the nature of money that its value—its desirability as a store of wealth—varies inversely with its availability relative to need. As the American deficit persisted, confidence in the dollar inevitably began to wane. But the instinctive reactions of European monetary authorities hardly explain why European governments did not choose to make greater use of their dollars by allowing them to be invested in real economic resources (by liberalizing imports, for example), where they could earn high returns in economic growth, rather than in gold. As Walter Salant put it in 1964, "In the immediate situation, where there is deficient [internal] demand in the main deficit country, the United States, and the surplus countries are threatened with inflation, a rational economic solution is perfectly elementary; the situations of the two groups of countries fit together perfectly. All four problems—the output gap in the United States, the excess demand in Western Europe, the deficit in the United States, and the surplus in Western Europe—could be reduced or eliminated if Western Europe, instead of accumulating nonearning assets in the form of reserves, would reduce its restrictions on imports, increase its contributions to collective defense, or increase its untied aid to underdeveloped countries." [7] Rational and elementary, perhaps, but not from the standpoint of European interests as continental Europeans see them.

Central to the continental view is the fear of inflation. Herman J. Abs, head of the Deutsche Bank and probably the most influential member of the German financial community, noted that Secretary of the Treasury Fowler's proposal (in July 1965) for a conference on monetary reform had been received on the Continent "with a certain reserve," because "these countries of necessity were more concerned with combating inflation than with the shortage of international liquidity that would arise from a United States balance-of-payments surplus." Particularly in Germany, Abs continued, "the fear of inflationary developments was greater than the fear that business activity might ease to a slower tempo." [8] This preoccupation with inflation is the consequence both of historical experience and of current economic conditions. The attitudes of

[7] *Does the International Monetary System Need Reform?* cited, p. 26.
[8] *The New York Times,* July 24, 1965.

continental Europeans were probably more profoundly affected by postwar inflation in the 1920s and 1940s than by deflation in the 1930s, which was less severe in Europe than in the United States. Their economies tend to have an excess of demand as well as a persistent price-wage spiral even when demand is not excessive.

The continental authorities' preferred method of coping with inflation is a restrictive monetary policy. The influx of American capital which has been so largely responsible for the dollar deficit therefore seems a mixed blessing. Valuable as it may be for Europe's growth, it tends to bring European interest rates down and to limit the effectiveness of European central bankers' efforts to deal with inflation by restricting bank credit. Any suggestion from Americans that capital inflow may be owing to the attraction of high interest rates is met by the argument that American interest rates are too low and ought to be raised. Continental authorities are apt to see the dollar problem as a manifestation of a too liberal credit policy in the United States. In their view, the dollar problem is an American problem and it is up to the United States to correct it.

Americans may reply that lower EEC tariffs and a less protectionist Common Agricultural Policy would also combat European inflation and reduce the deficit, to the general benefit of Europe and America, whereas restriction of domestic credit and of capital exports by this country could be inimical to growth at home and abroad. But this reasoning, however persuasive it has been to some Americans, has little appeal on the Continent today. It reckons without continental views on inflation and monetary policy. It cuts across economic and political interests which support agricultural and industrial protectionism. Nor is there much disposition in Europe to assume a larger share of the cost of maintaining the American forces in Germany. Europeans reason that these forces contribute as much to American as to European security and are not likely to be withdrawn simply for balance-of-payments reasons.

In furtherance of their preferred monetary strategy (and in France's case for more strictly political reasons as well), the continental governments and central banks have applied a good deal of pressure on the United States to do something about the dollar problem. Their pressure has been relatively effective—in part because their basic bargaining position is strong, in part because the firm American commitment to sell gold at thirty-five dollars an ounce provides an efficient lever by which to apply their power. Because their balance-of-payments position is reasonably good, because their reserves are high, and because they are able (even anxious) to do without some of the American capital they have been getting, their bargaining power has proved adequate to the purpose.

The American financial authorities continued for some time to hope that the balance of payments would soon come right through improvement of the trade and commercial balance, and as a result of the measures taken in the years 1960–62 to reduce the dollar drain of foreign aid and military spending. But gains from these sources were soon offset by the increasing outflow of capital. An attempt was then made to persuade European governments to hold more dollars in the form of special nonnegotiable claims ("Roosa bonds") and other relatively illiquid forms. Finally, when it became clear that the current account would not improve rapidly enough to correct the deficit, the Kennedy and Johnson administrations felt compelled to take direct action to reduce capital exports, in order to stem the gold drain and bolster European bankers' waning confidence in the dollar: a tax on foreign loans and on purchases of foreign securities, and "voluntary" export quotas on bank loans and direct investments. Thus the United States government was forced by the dollar deficit, by European pressure, and by its own unwillingness to adopt a restrictive monetary policy and to cut overseas spending, to restrict the foreign activities of American banks, industrial corporations, and investors, and to retreat from an objective it had long cherished: increasing freedom of international capital movements.

American opinion on the dollar problem is rather more divided than continental opinion. There is little disposition to quarrel with the need to take emergency measures to stem the outflow of gold; there is general agreement that these measures are highly undesirable in the longer run. Nevertheless, there is substantial disagreement about how seriously to take the dollar problem and what more to do about it.

One view, widely shared in business and financial circles, is that given Europe's unwillingness to accumulate more dollars, the United States ought to act more vigorously to defend the dollar, by a tighter monetary policy and by trimming foreign aid and military spending. According to this view, there is no shortage of international liquidity at this time to finance the American or any other deficit; the deficit ought to be corrected, not financed.[9]

Another view is held by many American economists and officials. It is that the deficit will probably correct itself within a few years, because European prices and costs are rising relative to American, with the consequence that the United States' trade balance will improve while Europe's deteriorates. Meanwhile, no further major measures to correct the deficit are necessary or desirable. Instead, attention should be focused on finding ways to finance it—particularly on international monetary reform. The critical element in the deficit, the outflow of capital, is inherently desirable, for the United States and for the world. Under the normal operations of the international monetary system it was financed automatically. Now that European resistance makes this impossible, there is need

---

[9] For a lucid statement of this view, see Emilio G. Collado, "The Future of the International Monetary System," *Gold, the Dollar and the World Monetary System* (New York: Committee for Economic Development, June 1965), p. 25.

for a new method of creating international liquidity. A more restrictive domestic monetary policy is undesirable. It would mean slower growth and more unemployment at home. It might put pressure on the payments of innocent bystanders: Britain, Japan, Canada, and underdeveloped countries, which would ultimately be harmful to American interests.[10]

As these words are written (January 1966) the sharpness of this disagreement, particularly as it relates to domestic credit policy, has been lessened by the emergence of inflationary pressure in the United States, owing, in part, to the sharp rise in military expenditures for the war in Vietnam. Nevertheless, a basic cleavage of opinion about the dollar problem and what to do about it persists.

The Question of Control

Whatever one may think of these two views, it seems clear that from an American standpoint the best solution of the dollar problem (given Europe's unwillingness to reduce import barriers drastically, to invest more abroad, and to increase military and aid expenditures) would be for European central banks to go on accumulating dollars in amounts sufficient to permit American restrictions on capital exports to be lifted. This would be best, too, for third countries, which are already feeling the pinch of the American restrictions. In time the deficit would probably correct itself, mainly through the continued relative rise of European costs and its effect on the commercial balance and on the profitability of European opportunities for American investment.

But the continental European financial authorities do not want the deficit corrected in this fashion. To them it would spell not only more inflation but also a loss of control of their domestic monetary conditions. If a large inflow of dollars were

[10] See, for example, Walter S. Salant, *A New Look at the U.S. Balance of Payments* (Washington: The Brookings Institution, 1965), pp. 19–23.

allowed to continue, a European country's balance of payments and its domestic credit base would be, to a considerable extent, under Washington's control. Continental central bankers are uneasy about their dollar holdings less because they fear that the United States might reduce the gold parity of the dollar (a remote risk) than because they fear the loss of control over domestic monetary conditions (a present danger). By refusing credit to the United States (which is the effect of converting dollars into gold) they preserve their monetary autonomy.

When a large economy is closely integrated with a smaller economy which is more dependent on foreign trade, a payments imbalance between them tends to be corrected by adjustments of costs and prices in the smaller economy.[11] At least this is what occurs (with fixed exchange rates) if the adjustment process is allowed to work itself out naturally without the imposition of controls. The process presupposes a ready source of international money to finance the deficit in the interim. This is, for example, the relationship between the American and Canadian economies, where freedom of capital movements provides the needed financing. It was also the case for continental European countries and the United States as long as the dollar deficit was self-financing.

If the continental governments continued on that basis, they would be allowing the American financial authorities to exert a determining influence on European prices, costs, and monetary conditions. As with nuclear power, so with the power of money. Atlantic integration tends to mean that the power and policies of the United States predominate. But with respect to money, unlike defense, European governments have real bargaining power because they have an alternative to American control: they can assert a degree of monetary autonomy by refusing or limiting the extension of credit to the United States. In the Canadian case, no such political issue is

[11] Mundell, cited, pp. 16–19.

raised, because Canada has been willing to accept monetary dependency as the price of a very high degree of economic integration with the United States, from which Canadian industry and commerce have greatly benefited. The hard core of the dollar problem is, then, political; it has to do with power and control.

It can be political, too, in a stricter sense: as De Gaulle has shown, the assertion of monetary autonomy can serve the cause of France's political autonomy. Just as De Gaulle attacks the credibility of the American nuclear guarantee, so he attacks the credit of the dollar. The objective in both cases, as far as the French president is concerned, is more strictly political than functional: to reduce American prestige and influence in Europe in the interest of France's freedom of action and his own design for Europe.

It is not surprising in the circumstances that some Americans are looking for ways to restore America's freedom of action in monetary matters and to enhance its bargaining power. Proposals have been made by several American economists [12] that the United States should wrest the gold lever from its European allies by the simple expedient of demonetizing gold, in whole or in part. As a technical matter this could be achieved unilaterally by qualifying or eliminating the American commitment to convert foreign official holdings of dollars into gold at thirty-five dollars an ounce. The attractiveness of gold as a reserve asset depends very largely on the assurance of its command over dollars, or American economic resources, at the guaranteed price. By a unilateral act the United States could thus make gold less desirable than the dollar and make the dollar again the only generally useful reserve asset.[13]

[12] See, e.g., *The New York Times*, May 30, 1965.
[13] Serious proposals to demonetize gold include a provision to preserve the economic value of foreign gold reserves existing on the date of the announcement— by allowing them to be converted into dollars or dollar claims at the thirty-five dollar rate, for example.

The proponents of demonetizing gold go on to point out that if it were not required to convert foreign official dollar holdings into gold at a guaranteed price, the United States government could spend abroad, limited only by considerations of domestic convenience and national advantage, while American corporations and banks could lend and invest abroad much as they do at home, limited only by business considerations and the credit-worthiness of borrowers. The underlying assumption is that if European financial authorities are deprived of the right to convert dollars into gold at a guaranteed price, they will either hold more dollars, or will take constructive measures to reduce their payments surplus— cutting tariffs, lowering interest rates, or increasing capital exports and foreign aid, for example.

The assumption is rather implausible politically. It reckons without the manifest unwillingness of European governments and central banks to be so largely subjected to the financial power of the United States Treasury and Federal Reserve Board. Whether or not that power were responsibly exercised in the general interest (let us presume it would be), the time is past when European governments could accept a reduction in their monetary autonomy. Although deprived of the leverage of gold, they would not be without means of defending their autonomy. They could, for example, restrict the inflow of American capital (by discriminatory taxes or exchange control), thus defeating the American objective of eliminating the balance-of-payments constraint on capital exports.

In the nuclear field, the United States may possibly still be able through new Atlantic nuclear arrangements to strengthen its hold on the strategy of the Alliance. In the monetary field this is not the case. The United States simply lacks the power to impose on its Atlantic allies a monetary system which would drastically increase the influence of the United States over the creation of international money. An attempt to do so would sharpen the present conflict of interests. It would impair the prospects for a cooperative approach to international monetary reform.

If proposals to demonetize gold express American interests in an extreme form, the French government's proposal to return to a modified form of gold standard is an equally extreme expression of continental interests. Although the French proposal has never been presented to the public in its entirety, it apparently has the following elements.[14] All existing official dollar balances would be converted by the United States government into gold at thirty-five dollars an ounce. Thereafter settlements among central banks would be either entirely in gold, or partly in gold and partly in a new international monetary unit, in an agreed ratio. The new unit (the CRU or Collective Reserve Unit) would be created outside the IMF from time to time by unanimous agreement of the principal financial powers. It would be distributed to participating countries in proportion to their gold reserves. CRUs and gold would be used for settlements between central banks in such a way as to preserve an agreed CRU-gold ratio in national reserves.

An arrangement of this kind would tend to eliminate the dollar as a reserve asset, in favor of gold and CRUs. It would link the creation of additional international liquidity closely to gold reserves and make the total amount of CRUs and any change in the gold-CRU ratios subject to the *liberum veto* of the continental governments. The dollar would no doubt re-

[14] A public statement of the French position was given by Minister of Finance Valery Giscard d'Estaing in a lecture at the Sorbonne on February 11, 1965 (mimeographed). The Minister's lecture was apparently intended to explain and qualify President de Gaulle's dramatic assertion in his February 4, 1965, press conference, "that international exchanges must be established, as was the case before the great world-wide disasters, on an unquestionable monetary basis which does not bear the mark of any individual country. What basis? Actually, it is difficult to envision in this regard any other criterion, any other standard than gold." Ambassade de France, Speeches and Press Conferences, No. 216, p. 6. The Ossola Report contains a statement of those parts of the French plan which relate to the creation and distribution of new reserve assets. *Report of the Study Group on the Creation of Reserve Assets,* May 31, 1965, pp. 26–29.

main the principal vehicle currency (there is nothing to replace it), but its use as a reserve asset and for international settlements would be drastically curtailed. In sum, the French proposal would closely link the expansion of international liquidity to gold holdings and make it subject to the unanimous agreement of the principal financial powers.[15]

A system of this kind would be too biased in the direction of credit restriction and too destructive of the natural reserve currency role of the dollar and sterling to work in a manner satisfactory to the United States or Britain, or most other non-European countries, unless there were a great deal more international agreement than there is on monetary strategy and liquidity requirements. And if there were such agreement, it would be neither necessary nor wise to establish a system whose natural tendency would be to link the growth of reserves to the slow growth of gold holdings.

In political terms, the gold-biased French proposal is as far out of line with the present balance of power in monetary affairs as are proposals for the demonetization of gold. Neither the United States, Britain, Canada, Japan, nor even some of France's EEC neighbors could concede to France an absolute veto on the creation of international money. Indeed it seems probable that the French plan has been advanced not as a serious basis for negotiation but as a tactical maneuver to establish a strong bargaining posture and to assert French independence.

The Sterling Problem

Europe's reaction to American financial power is responsible for one major cleavage in Atlantic monetary relations. Britain's financial weakness is the cause of another. The conti-

---

[15] Thus the French proposal is for a gold standard in only the special sense that gold would be the principal or controlling reserve asset. The French government does not propose a return to the mechanical link of the traditional gold standard between gold reserves and domestic credit.

nental governments are reluctant to join the United States in the regular creation of new international money, because they fear it would mean more inflation and less autonomy. They are equally reluctant to do so with Britain, for fear of reducing the pressure on the British government to do something fundamental about the British balance of payments. They fear, not without reason, that to create more reserves for Britain would amount to giving the British unrequited aid.

Sterling is weak because Britain's competitive position in export markets is chronically weak. The causes have been apparent for the last decade or more; they are fundamental and closely related to the chronically slow rate of Britain's economic growth.[16] Slow growth means that wages tend to rise faster relative to productivity than in more dynamic economies, driving British labor costs and export prices up faster than those of other industrial countries. Moreover, the economic climate in a slow-growing economy is uncongenial to the vigorous, innovating kind of industrial management which is essential for competitive strength in a world where industrial competition takes increasingly the form of new products and technologies. The story of slow growth and overly conservative management is a very old one in Britain, whose economy has been relatively undynamic since World War I. The deficient vigor of British management and its implications for exports have been of concern to British governments since the 1920s.

External factors, too, have played a part. As the first power to industrialize, Britain's exports were more concentrated in the older industries, such as textiles, in which world trade has been relatively stagnant, and in former colonies and dominions where tariffs are particularly restrictive (India and Australia, for example). And because British industry is so

[16] See Alfred Maizels, *Industrial Growth and World Trade* (London: Cambridge University Press, 1963), pp. 217–224, Wilfred Beckerman, "Projecting Europe's Growth," *The Economic Journal* (December 1962), pp. 916–917; Elliott, Cleveland and Geiger, cited, pp. 85–86, 97–108.

heavily dependent on export markets, the slow growth of exports owing to all these factors reinforces the internal causes of slow economic growth.

Britain's reserve position is woefully weak. Its short-term official obligations to the United States, the IMF and the Group of Ten (under the General Agreement to Borrow) now exceed its owned reserves. Britain, indeed, is the only developed country which has a major existing, as distinguished from a potential future, shortage of liquidity.

Finally, the weakness of the balance of payments is itself a major obstacle to growth. The need frequently to resort to a restrictive fiscal and monetary policy which has been the unavoidable response of successive British governments to recurrent balance-of-payments strain and weak reserve position has held back industrial investment and discouraged innovative zeal. "In the United Kingdom, although the average *pressure* of demand over the whole [postwar] period has not been low by international standards, experience has taught all but the most ill-informed entrepreneurs that, however high may be the *rate of growth* of demand in the short run, it will not persist, since the external balance soon deteriorates, thereby requiring measures of demand restraint." [17]

Heroic domestic measures of great political difficulty are needed to break out of this complex of vicious circles: an effective incomes policy (keeping wage increases in line with productivity—something which has so far eluded all Western governments); more effective incentives to management; a redirection of government spending and investment.[18] Easier access to the markets of the European Economic Community and full membership if that proves to be possible might make the critical difference, as we shall see in the following chapter.

Meanwhile, the problem will persist. Indeed, the familiar

[17] Beckerman, cited, p. 917. (Italics in original.)

[18] The Wilson government's comprehensive economic plan, published September 16, 1965, contains these and many other elements. It remains to be seen how far they can be carried out. *The National Plan*, Cmd. 2764, London, September 1965.

dilemma of growth or external balance is likely to worsen. A recent authoritative analysis reaches the bleak conclusion that "without a substantial change in past relationships, either between imports and national output, or between British exports and world trade in manufactures, the objectives of righting the balance of payments and of full employment and reasonable growth seem quite incompatible." [19] Import restrictions, such as the "temporary" 15 per cent surcharge on imports imposed in October 1964 (reduced to 10 per cent in April 1965), are quite likely to be a continuing feature of British policy, at least for the near future. Foreign military and aid expenditures and foreign investment will have to be reduced.

Britain, therefore, is likely for some years yet to remain a relatively unattractive partner from Europe's standpoint in any scheme for the regular expansion of monetary reserves. The United States, however, for political reasons is more unambiguously interested than the main continental powers in Britain's economic welfare. American and British interests in international monetary reform are also reasonably parallel. Both countries would be best served by a system which provided easier access to new international money than Europe is now willing to contemplate. Thus Americans are inclined to see the sterling problem more as a reason for monetary reform (along these lines) than as an obstacle to it. Monetary and political interests tend to align Britain and America against the leading continental powers in international monetary affairs.

Shared Control or Disintegration?

The Atlantic economy is too integrated in financial terms to work in the future as well as it worked in the past, unless the principal governments can agree on a new way of expand-

<hr />

[19] See *National Institute Economic Review* (London: National Institute of Economic and Social Research, August 1965), p. 17.

ing periodically the supply of international money. It must be a new way, because the old way has implications for continental Europe's monetary autonomy which are no longer acceptable, and because Europe has the financial power to make its resistance effective. The need of the Atlantic nations for more reserves may not be so urgent as is sometimes asserted, but if it does not yet exist (except in Britain's case) it will and probably soon. If agreement on a new way is not forthcoming, the result sooner or later is likely to be a reduction in the degree of Atlantic economic integration—a further reduction, rather; the restrictions on American capital exports are already a substantial retreat.

We are not among the monetary Cassandras who now prophesy that without a major reform the present system is headed for a spectacular collapse of credit precipitated, perhaps, by a new wave of speculation against sterling followed by a run on the American gold stock. The 1960s are not the 1930s. There is today a working consensus among the Atlantic governments and Japan that they will cooperate to protect the system from speculative pressures and financial panic, as the successive multilateral support operations for sterling have shown. Moreover, governments today are committed to maintain domestic demand, which loosens the link between internal credit and the balance of payments. A general shortage of international liquidity, should one develop, is therefore unlikely to produce a cumulative downward spiral of demand as in the 1930s.

Not spectacular collapse but a creeping growth of capital restrictions, restrictive pressure on internal monetary policies, and a slower growth of trade and production would be the eventual consequence of a stalemate on monetary reform. Any prolonged pause in the rapid expansion of international trade which the non-Communist world has enjoyed since 1945, and any widespread reimposition of payments restrictions owing to spreading balance-of-payments trouble, would be a setback to aims which have cost the United States and its Atlantic allies much treasure and immense diplomatic effort. The Atlantic Community does not need international monetary reform to prevent an impending disaster, but it does need it to help safeguard the accomplishments of two decades of foreign economic policy.

Shared control is the essential ingredient of international monetary reform. The existing monetary system will doubtless continue to function in the future as it has in the past for much of the trading world. But the principal continental governments have made it clear that no source of new reserves (apart from gold) whose control they do not fully share will be acceptable. No international money will find its way into their official reserves unless they have shared in the creating of it. As Pierre Paul Schweitzer, managing director of the IMF put it, "The creation of international liquidity, like the creation of domestic liquidity, should become a matter of deliberate decision." [20]

The difficulty is that sharing control of international money, like sharing control of nuclear weapons, presupposes a consensus on strategy and objectives. Plainly, no consensus is in prospect sufficiently wide and deep to support an international monetary agency with discretionary power to create money and distribute it according to policies made, for example, by majority vote of the member governments. Even if it could be established, such a "superbank" would be quite unable to function. As Robert Roosa once put it, "It would be inescapable, so long as major differences in economic policy arise among different countries, that those differences will prevent the systematic direction of the superbank on uniform and consistent lines. The outcome, if it is not utter chaos and impairment of normal payments transactions among nations, is likely instead to be a drifting back toward systems of reliance

[20] Quoted in *The Economist* (London), February 6, 1965, p. 567.

upon clusters of currencies, and dependence on the strength given them by the economies which underlie them." [21]

The power to create or withhold international money is the power to use a nation's economic resources in ways and for purposes it might not choose itself. It is the power to transmit inflation or deflation from one country to another. It is the power to influence local conditions of demand and employment. The Atlantic governments can hardly delegate such powers to any majority of their number. Sharing, if it comes about, will take a far more modest form. New reserve assets will be created by unanimous consent of (at least) the principal financial powers. They will be distributed in accordance with a simple "across-the-board" formula, such as that by which increased quotas in the IMF have been allocated.

The principal Atlantic governments now apparently agree that a new reserve asset of some kind is needed and that it should be created and distributed in some such manner as this. What they disagree about is more fundamental, however. They disagree about whether action is needed now or at some unspecified future time. They disagree about how much of the total process of reserve creation should be subject to collective control. France, with considerable support from her EEC partners, wants to subject the entire process to collective control. That is the purpose of the tight gold link of the French plan. The United States, with British support, wants to limit collective control to the creation of reserve assets which would merely supplement other processes of reserve creation —particularly the accumulation of dollar and sterling balances by countries willing to do so. Thus the United States seeks to defend its financial power and freedom of action while providing a means of financing imbalances which continental countries will honor.

[21] Federal Reserve Bank of Philadelphia, *Business Review Supplement* (September 1962), reprinted in Henry G. Grubel, ed., *World Monetary Reform* (Stanford University Press, 1963), p. 269.

As this is written, prospects for an eventual reconciliation of the opposed positions are not discouraging. Despite conflicts of monetary objectives and (in France's case) of more strictly political objectives as well, none of the major Atlantic countries seems to contemplate with equanimity the possibility (however remote it may seem) of a widespread resort to payments restrictions, such as would be the probable result of a real liquidity shortage. Agreement to some kind of supplementary reserve asset or assets, created and distributed in the manner just described, may therefore be forthcoming in time.

If this prognosis proves too optimistic and the present deadlock on reform persists indefinitely, the United States might in time have to join with countries with which it could agree in an effort to limit the adverse consequences of a developing shortage of liquidity. This possibility is implicit already in the exemption of Canada and (in part) Japan from the United States' interest equalization tax, and in the large swap arrangement with Britain. The logical tendency of this line of development is toward a monetary system consisting of two main groupings: a dollar group including the United States, Britain, Canada, Japan, Latin America, Australia, New Zealand, and possibly some EFTA countries, with the sterling area as a subgroup; a continental group including the Six and countries whose trade relations are predominantly with the Six: Austria, Switzerland, Greece, Turkey, and much of Africa.

Such groupings would not be "currency blocs" in the sense of the interwar years. They would be groups of countries which keep their currencies closely aligned and which are willing to extend each other sufficient credit to maintain a relatively higher degree of financial integration within the group. Between the groups, settlements would tend to be made largely in gold, and payments balance would be maintained in part by restrictions on imports and capital movements.

A division of the Atlantic world into currency blocs would

obviously be less desirable from an American standpoint than an international monetary reform which made it possible to preserve the present degree of financial integration, if this could be done without an intolerable sacrifice of American freedom of action in monetary affairs. For Britain, too, the erection of a new currency barrier between herself and the continental Six would impede the growth of her exports and impair still further her prospects for "joining Europe." It would be only as a last resort, to mitigate the consequences of a failure of the Atlantic nations to agree on how to bring about an orderly expansion of the supply of international money, that a two-bloc arrangement might seem desirable, on the ground that it would be better than the unorganized response of governments to a pervasive shortage of international funds.[22]

Sooner or later the Atlantic nations will have to choose between maintaining a high degree of financial integration with the aid of a substantial additional source of international money created by multilateral agreement, and a partial disintegration of their international economic system. The interests and inclinations of the United States clearly make the first choice the better one by far.

[22] See, for example, Salant and Despres, cited, pp. 258–262, and Mundell, cited, pp. 58–63.

CHAPTER FOUR

Trade Policy

The observer who turns from Atlantic monetary to trade questions is at once aware that the problems are less pressing and divisive. In part this is because trade policy today is inherently less important in economic terms than monetary policy. How international monetary arrangements work, or fail to work, can affect levels of employment and rates of growth throughout the trading world. Trade-policy decisions today have much more limited economic consequences. The progress which the industrial countries have made since the war in adopting international rules about trade policy—in particular, the General Agreement on Tariffs and Trade—and in liberalizing trade serves to contain disagreements about trade policy within a narrower range than is true of monetary matters.

Nevertheless, controversy about trade-policy questions within the Atlantic Community is on the rise. As in military and monetary matters, the principal contending parties are the United States and the members of the European Economic Community. The main issue is the Community's external trade policy.

The agreement of the Six to form a customs union with a common external tariff and a common agricultural policy has created a formidable new trading bloc which alters radically the balance of trading power in the Atlantic economic community. The United States, having armed itself for the first time in many years with effective tariff-cutting authority, is pressing for more rapid general trade liberalization under the standard of the Most-Favored-Nation Principle (MFN). The European Community is resisting—in part on simple protectionist grounds, in part for fear of losing its newly won trade bargaining power, in part for more strictly political reasons: the significance of its common external tariff and agricultural policy, the principal concrete achievements of the European idea, will be reduced if the United States has its way.

Meanwhile, the frustrations of the Kennedy Round of tariff negotiations have caused Americans to raise fundamental questions about the direction of American trade policy. Is multilateral tariff negotiation obsolete? Has MFN outlived its usefulness? Should both be replaced by a new approach to trade liberalization which would absorb the European Community into a great Atlantic free-trade system, or by-pass it in favor of preferential agreements with Britain and other industrial countries?

We shall return to these questions in the latter part of this chapter, but first a little background is necessary.

Trade Policy in the 1950s

The postwar trade arrangements among the Atlantic nations were the result of an effort by the United States to reverse the protectionist tide which ran so strongly in the 1930s and to restore a relatively integrated international economy among nations able and willing to participate. At the war's end, the United States, its power and prestige at a peak, was able to persuade its Atlantic neighbors to adopt the General Agreement on Tariffs and Trade, the GATT. It codified the most liberal features of the network of trade agreements which had defined the world trading system before 1914, and defined certain exceptions to these principles. The GATT had two objectives: one was nondiscrimination; the other trade liberalization. The former was implemented by the MFN principle; the latter by outlawing trade barriers (other than ordinary tariffs) except import quotas imposed temporarily for balance-of-payments reasons, and by providing for periodic multilateral negotiation of agreements to reduce duties.

Commercial interests and political concerns led the United States to assume this role. The commercial interest of the largest and most competitive trading nation lay in the general opening of world markets and the dismantling of the British and French colonial preferences. The American officials responsible for trade policy in the 1940s were also motivated by a larger and more political concern: the contribution which freer trade could make to the world's economic health and political stability. Some believed in the Cobdenite notion that freer trade would of itself bring international understanding. GATT and the stillborn International Trade Organization were not considered instruments of foreign policy in the usual sense. At this time there was little conscious concern for American political interests in the narrower sense (power and prestige), and "economic foreign policy" and "political foreign policy" occupied two separate compartments in the American diplomatic establishment.

The American effort met with considerable success. One reason was that the United States had the power to induce other countries to accept the essentials of its conception. Another was that the main prewar causes of protectionism had disappeared.

The extreme protectionism of the 1930s had several causes. Developments in the economic organization of Western society had brought into being politically powerful organizations of producers—industrialists, labor unions, farmers' organizations—seeking the assistance of the state to advance their interests and protect them from foreign competition. The origin of these new forces goes back well before World War I. But it was only under the impact of general deflation, mass unemployment, and collapsing farm prices, and the accompanying disillusionment with *laissez faire,* that the protectionists were able wholly to get their way, as governments strove desperately to shift the impact of deflation to foreigners.

Protectionism in the 1930s was further reinforced by the attempt of the larger European states and Japan to increase their economic self-sufficiency for military reasons. World War I had demonstrated that in a total war of attrition, the ability to withstand enemy blockade could be critical. Thus the pursuit of self-sufficiency (for military purposes) combined with protectionism (born of depression) to destroy the integrated trading system which had prevailed until 1914.

Neither factor has been present in the postwar period. Demand has been buoyant and employment high, owing, in part, no doubt, to the common determination of the industrial countries to avoid deflation. The military case for protectionism is obsolete. The Atlantic Community is a security community. War among Atlantic nations or between them and Japan is hardly conceivable, at least as long as they face the common danger of Soviet or Chinese power and ambition. The security of the West and Japan depends not on their capacity to fight a war of attrition and to withstand naval blockade, but on their ability to mount in peacetime nuclear forces adequate to neutralize the nuclear forces of the Soviet Union. This ability is enhanced by the more rapid industrial growth and greater access to foreign capital and technology which come with freer trade. In a nuclear age, national self-sufficiency would tend to reduce military security rather than to increase it.

The relative success of trade liberalization has also been the result of growing support from management and labor in the industrial countries. Trade liberalization has created vested interests in its own continuation, at least within the industrial sector. Many thousands of business decisions made on the expectation that tariffs will be stable or declining have gradually changed the interests and attitudes of industrialists and labor leaders about tariff policy. Given the more or less steady expansion of world demand for manufactures, trade liberalization in the industrial sector has been self-reinforcing.

Marked changes in the structure of international trade in manufactures have reduced the relative importance of tariffs and helped to shift the balance of interests within the Atlantic industrial community toward freer world trade. World trade has expanded much more rapidly in product categories where protection has traditionally been lower—machinery, transport equipment, and many chemicals, for example—because, at higher levels of national income, demand for these products grows faster than for other manufactures.[1] At higher levels of national income, moreover, a larger proportion of manufactures consists of novel consumer goods and highly specialized capital equipment, which compete in international trade on the basis of uniqueness, quality, or service rather than price. For such manufactures, tariffs are often of little importance.

Tariff cutting, moreover, had time to gather momentum without any immediate impact on import-competing industries in the United States, because of the temporary eclipse of Europe's industrial power. Similarly, Europe's shortage of foreign exchange and consequent need to retain quantitative restrictions on imports for balance-of-payments reasons meant that the impact of tariff cutting was quite limited in Europe, too, until the general restoration of currency convertibility and the removal of most import quotas in 1958–1959. Thus GATT's principles and the practice of regular tariff cutting had time to become well established before protectionists in Europe or the United States had much to complain about.

There has been, in short, a change in the balance of forces

[1] See Alfred Maizels, *Industrial Growth and World Trade* (London: Cambridge University Press, for the National Institute of Economic and Social Research, 1963), p. 179.

as between protectionists and partisans of free trade, in the industrial sector at any rate. The most prestigeful and politically powerful elements of the Atlantic business community have been converted to trade liberalization. One has only to think of the trade philosophy of the Committee for Economic Development, the United States Chamber of Commerce, the Bundesoverband Deutscher Industrie, or *mirabile dictu* the French Patronat, to appreciate how great the change since 1939 has been.

Nevertheless, tariff cutting among the Atlantic countries in the 1940s and 1950s was relatively modest. Since the United States set the pace for all, the President's rather restricted authority under the Trade Agreements Act meant that tariff cutting had to be moderate, and quite selective. A series of restrictive amendments to the act sponsored by protectionist interests further reduced the freedom of action of the executive branch in tariff negotiations and tended to focus tariff cutting on products where the effect on trade was least.

Still, a great many industrial tariffs were cut in the course of four rounds of negotiations. The direct effects on trade may not have been large,[2] but the effect of the sustained downward trend of tariff rates on exporters' confidence and willingness to expand sales abroad must have been very substantial. No doubt the stability of exchange rates has also contributed to this result.[3]

[2] Don D. Humphrey, *The United States and the Common Market* (New York: Praeger, 1962), pp. 51–53.

[3] Alfred Maizels's study of world trade in manufactures brings out the over-all effect of postwar trade liberalization and removal of currency restrictions on the growth of trade among the industrial countries. He shows that by the end of the 1950s the relationship between the growth of trade in manufactures among the industrial countries and the growth of their total output of manufactures had reverted to the "normal" relationship which prevailed from 1899 to 1929, but which was altered by trade and currency restrictions in the 1930s. In his words, "The long-term movement in world trade in manufactures has been closely related to that in world manufacturing production. There was a break in the relationship in the 1930s, but in historical perspective this appears as a discontinuity due to special factors (trade and currency restrictions) which depressed the level of trade in those years." Cited, p. 11. This result reflects not only the direct and indirect effect of tariff cuts, but also (more importantly) the removal of quantitative restrictions.

Trade liberalization has been confined to the industrial sector, however. Little or no liberalization has occurred in agriculture; indeed, the trend has been the other way.[4] In all the industrial countries the technological revolution has finally reached agriculture, and the productivity of agricultural labor is rising rapidly. The movement of labor out of farming and into other employment, although rapid by historical standards, is not happening quickly enough to prevent food production from outstripping consumption. The financial burden of surplus food production in the United States, Canada, and France, the principal net food exporters, grows heavier, while the net food-importing countries supply a growing part of their needs domestically. Given the disproportionate political influence of farmers, the result is a growing network of price supports, subsidies, import quotas, and tariffs whose purpose is to insulate farm prices and farmers' incomes from market forces, domestic and foreign.

Yet the industrial countries are rich, and many of them have small farm populations. They can afford the political luxury of supporting more farmers than would be necessary to feed their populations if the Atlantic agricultural economy were more integrated. Despite an occasional chicken war, and sporadic attempts to negotiate about agricultural trade, the Atlantic governments seem to have tacitly agreed that trade liberalization does not really apply to agriculture. This was true at any rate until 1963, when the United States made a serious effort to obtain agricultural concessions in the Kennedy Round of tariff negotiations—an attempt which is unlikely to meet with marked success.

Even within the industrial sector certain industries in which the total volume of trade has been stagnant, in which international competition has been particularly severe, and for which tariffs have traditionally been high, have been largely

[4] The causes of this trend are examined by John O. Coppock in his *Atlantic Agricultural Unity: Is It Possible?* (New York: McGraw-Hill, for the Council on Foreign Relations, 1966.)

excluded from the general liberalizing trend. Textiles and clothing are the principal examples. In 1962 the principal industrial countries signed a formal agreement whose effect is to keep their imports of cotton textiles within prescribed quantitative limits. The Cotton Textile Agreement is an official market-sharing arrangement whose purpose is to limit international competition.

In sum, America's postwar efforts to establish a more integrated trading system among industrial countries met with considerable success, because the prewar causes of extreme industrial protectionism had disappeared, because the United States had the power to make its will effective, and because its objectives were moderate. The system involved a politically realistic balance between protectionism and integration. In economic sectors, where support for integration was absent because of governmental involvement in market control (agriculture) or the character of international competition (textiles), the Atlantic nations have in practice agreed that protectionism is better, or at least less trouble, than integration. Wealthy industrial countries can afford a certain amount of inefficiency in agriculture and the older industries for the sake of domestic peace. In other sectors trade liberalization has fed on itself. Private interests have supported the decision of governments to give up some autonomy in tariff policy in order to gain the assurance that the general trend of tariffs will be downward and that duties will not be arbitrarily raised.

Trade Liberalization and European Economic Integration

Nondiscriminatory trade liberalization was the initial aim of America's postwar trade policy, but regional economic integration in Europe soon became an equally if not more important objective. In principle, the two aims were hardly consistent. European economic integration meant discrimination by European countries in one another's favor and some diversion of trade from non-European to European sources. Yet this inconsistency did not at first give rise to any conflict of interest between Europe and the United States.

One reason was that European tariff discrimination was potential, not actual, until the dollar shortage ended and the first internal tariff cuts were made by the European Economic Community in 1959. With food production and industrial capacity in Europe still not recovered from the war, American exports, financed by a massive outpouring of aid dollars, dominated world markets throughout the 1950s. In these circumstances, export interests were little concerned about possible future European tariff discrimination. Further, the United States had long accepted European tariff discrimination in the form of a customs union or free-trade area as proper and even desirable.[5]

The strength of the political case for European unity was, however, the chief reason why European economic integration and multilateral trade liberalization were reconcilable in American as well as European eyes. The American sympathy for a European customs union was an earlier and less political

[5] The original draft of a charter of an International Trade Organization, proposed by the United States in 1946, contained an exemption from the most-favored-nation principle for customs unions which met certain conditions designed to assure that they would tend to have an expansive (trade-creating) rather than a restrictive (trade-diverting) effect on the members' trade with the rest of the world. The GATT contains substantially the same provision. It exempts from the general MFN requirement customs unions which eliminate duties on "substantially all" trade among the members, and whose common external tariff is "on the whole no higher or more restrictive" than the duties of the members as a group at the time they formed the union. Equivalent conditions apply to a parallel exemption for free-trade areas. A free-trade area, like a customs union, involves elimination of duties on trade among the members. It differs from a customs union in that the members do not have a common external tariff but retain full tariff autonomy with respect to their trade with nonmember countries. See Jacob Viner, *The Customs Union Issue* (New York: Carnegie Endowment for International Peace, 1950), p. 135. It will be recalled that in 1947 the Committee of European Economic Cooperation had proposed a European Customs Union Study Group, Committee of European Economic Cooperation, *General Report*, Paris, September 21, 1947 (U.S. Department of State Publication No. 2930) Vol. I, pp. 33–37. This proposal was made mainly because American officials insisted on it.

form of the same attitude. We shall consider in the next chapter the reasons for American support of the European idea. Union was needed to imprison Europe's evil genie, nationalism, in a solid federal cage. An objective of this high political importance outweighed any incidental damage to commercial interests. Even on a strictly commercial calculus, a united and dynamic European economy would be a better trading partner than the compartmentalized, stagnant European economy which then appeared to be the alternative if Europe failed to unite.

"The Challenge of the Common Market"

The Kennedy administration's proposal of the Trade Expansion Bill in January 1962 marks the point at which the harmony between general trade liberalization and European integration began to break down. The European Common Market, the central objective of American policy for more than a decade, had become, in the euphemism of the day, a "challenge"—that is, a problem. Henceforth the reconciliation of the two objectives and the economic and political interests they express would be the central issue of Atlantic trade policy.

The change in the American perception of the European Community came quite suddenly. Continental Europe's rapid economic recovery in the late 1950s and its continued economic dynamism had not been anticipated. Many Americans had believed that the Western European economy would remain stagnant and in chronic balance-of-payments trouble until integration had actually been achieved. With the signatures to the Treaty of Rome scarcely dry, many Americans were surprised to find a group of weak and dependent client states transformed into a formidable trading bloc, possessing the most rapidly growing internal market in the world and wielding, by virtue of a common external tariff and a volume of external trade greater than America's, more bargaining power in trade negotiations than the United States.

As the Six established their external tariff and began to reduce internal tariffs on an accelerated schedule, the magnitude of the trade diversion which would ultimately be involved began to be appreciated. As the Community began work on a common agricultural policy, it became apparent that to make agricultural integration politically feasible, food prices within the Community would have to be raised toward the levels prevailing in Germany, the high-cost producer. This was to be accomplished by flexible tariffs ("variable levies") on imports of food into the Community. The resulting system would be the most protectionist in the world (for a large area). Unless it could be substantially modified in the course of trade negotiations, there would be substantial trade diversion, an accelerated rise in European food production, and a corresponding reduction in imports, especially from North America. Thus European agricultural integration would be achieved at the expense of American and Canadian taxpayers, who would be required to support larger surpluses.

Meanwhile, Europe's dollar shortage had been replaced by the United States' balance-of-payments deficit. Trade diversion and increased agricultural protection in Europe were therefore not merely "challenges" to American commercial interests. They were threats to the dollar and to America's monetary autonomy.

Such considerations of national interest underlay the decision of the Kennedy administration to ask the Congress for a major increase in tariff-cutting authority. The purpose was to arm the executive with sufficient bargaining power vis-à-vis the EEC to prevent its external commercial policy being solidified in a protectionist mold. An "outward-looking" EEC had replaced European integration as the prime objective of American trade policy.

Considerations of power and control underlay this revision of priorities. The rise of a new European trading giant meant that the United States was in danger of losing its position of leadership in shaping the trade arrangements of the non-Communist world. During the 1940s and 1950s the United States had written the rules of the trade-policy game and determined the general pace of trade liberalization. In the 1960s the bargaining power of the Community would make that impossible. The EEC might use its power in ways inconsistent with American interests—for example, to establish preferential arrangements with other countries which would be detrimental to American commercial interests and to the interests of countries for which the United States has a special political responsibility, such as Japan and Latin America.

This consideration was a basic if seldom articulated motive of the Trade Expansion legislation. If the United States could no longer dominate the making of Atlantic trade policy, it could at least hope to persuade the Common Market to join an "Atlantic trade partnership" [6]—that is, to give up much of its tariff autonomy in return for a commitment by the United States to do likewise. In this way economic efficiency rather than bargaining power would determine the outcome of competition between the two leading trading powers. American policy makers felt confident, as they had throughout the post-war period, that in a liberal, multilateral trading regime American interests would not come off second best.

Thus the trading power of the EEC accomplished what a more diffuse and less political interest in trade liberalization had never been able to do: it persuaded an American Congress to adopt a truly liberal tariff law. Fear of the consequences of Europe's power, rather than a conversion to the principles of free trade, brought about this revolution in American policy.

---

[6] This expression was first used officially in President Kennedy's message to the Congress of January 11, 1962, requesting enactment of the Trade Expansion law.

The novel form of tariff-cutting authority contained in the "dominant-supplier" provision of the Trade Expansion Act underlines the American preoccupation with the EEC. The Act was intended to authorize tariff cutting to zero, on a reciprocal basis, for a long list of industrial categories which accounted for the bulk of the manufactured exports of the United States and the members (actual and prospective) of the Common Market. Had it been possible to conclude a United States–EEC trade agreement of the kind contemplated by this provision, tariff policy would have been largely removed from the agenda of major Atlantic problems, at least as to nonagricultural products.

Considerations of a more strictly political character also underlay the Trade Expansion Act. The Act was intended to put pressure on Britain to join the Community and on the Six to take her in. That was why the "dominant-supplier" provision was drafted in such a way as to be effective only if Britain joined. Full British participation in European unification had long been an American objective. Earlier, the principal motive had been concern about the political balance and democratic character of a European union. Now a concern about Europe's political orientation also made itself felt. British membership, it was hoped, would guarantee Europe's Atlantic orientation.[7] At first this new American concern was felt only vaguely.[8] After De Gaulle's veto of British membership in January 1963 Americans began to see the Common Market's trade policy as an index of the Community's political character. The Kennedy Round of tariff negotiations, which opened in May 1963, became in American eyes a test of the Community's loyalty to the Atlantic idea.

[7] See, Max Beloff, *The United States and the Unity of Europe* (Washington: The Brookings Institution, 1963), p. 101.

[8] It was expressed in statements that the Common Market would impair the "Political unity" or "cohesion" of the Atlantic Community unless its trade policy were "outward looking." See, for example, *A New Trade Policy for the United States,* a Statement on National Policy by The Research and Policy Committee of the Committee for Economic Development (New York: April 1962), p. 5.

On the other side of the Atlantic, the political content of trade policy was also increasing. American officials miscalculated in thinking that an "Atlantic trade partnership" would be attractive to the Six. The Six saw the drastic reduction or elimination of many industrial tariffs as a threat to their principal achievement as "Europeans": the customs union. Continental Europeans believed "that the elimination of duties would weaken the bonds holding together the countries of the Common Market, of which the common tariff is the principal outward manifestation. Moreover, several [European] commentators suggested that the United States' proposals were reminiscent of those made by Britain at the time when the United Kingdom wanted to dilute the EEC through the establishment of an all-European Free Trade Area." [9] The Six were also suspicious of the "dominant-supplier" principle. It seemed to favor the industries in which America's competitive power was superior to Europe's—the technologically advanced industries—and thus to endanger the development of such industries within the Community.[10]

In this way the Kennedy Round assumed a political character quite different from earlier rounds of tariff negotiations. It became more or less explicitly a contest between the European and Atlantic ideas.

This, too, is why the Kennedy Round has been widely assumed by Americans to be a failure, although the results are not yet in. As this is written, it is uncertain whether the negotiations will "succeed" or "fail," if the standard of comparison is previous negotiations. The Kennedy Round may yield cuts in industrial tariffs quite large compared with those agreed in earlier negotiations. Although it is true that the agricultural negotiation is likely to yield meager results,[11] this was also

[9] The quotation is from the manuscript of a book by Bela Balassa, to be published by McGraw-Hill, for the Council on Foreign Relations in 1967.

[10] Same.

[11] The President's tariff-cutting authority under the Trade Expansion Act will expire on June 30, 1967, unless the Congress extends it or grants other authority. For this reason, the administration has taken the position that the Kennedy Round should be concluded in 1966.

true of earlier attempts to reduce barriers to agricultural trade.

The nature of the Community's Common Agricultural Policy and the difficulty the Six have had in reaching agreement on it leave the Community little scope for trade liberalization. This is particularly true of products covered by the variable levy system, which include the major part of the Community's agricultural imports as well as those in which the American interest is concentrated (feed grains and dairy products). The variable levy is a tariff which is adjusted administratively by the EEC so as to restrict imports of agricultural products to a level which is consistent with maintaining predetermined "reference prices" (*prix indicatifs*) within the Community for products covered by the system. The system is designed to limit imports to the difference between consumption and what is produced within the Community at the reference price. The reference prices established by the Community are well above normal import prices and thus encourage increased production in the Community. They would therefore have to be reduced to allow imports to increase. The reference prices were the result of a long and difficult negotiation ending in a political compromise between Germany and France. They are unlikely to be substantially modified.

Furthermore, the United States, which has the largest export stake in the agricultural negotiation, has little bargaining power to make its interest effective. American imports of agricultural products from the Common Market are small. The United States cannot credibly threaten to withhold industrial concessions in order to gain agricultural concessions for the United States has more interest than the EEC in the success of the industrial negotiation.

But for some Americans the measures of success or failure in the Kennedy Round are not the results of previous negotiations. The criteria are the ambitious objectives of the Trade Expansion Act: to reduce drastically the degree of trade diversion involved in the Community's customs union; to reduce the Community's bargaining power in trade negotiations; to test and (hopefully) strengthen its Atlantic political orientation. According to those who hold this view, the Kennedy Round promises to fail, not in the sense that the trend of industrial trade liberalization will be permanently halted or reversed, but because the original American objectives will not be achieved.

The realism and relevance of this judgment may be doubted. Nevertheless, Americans disappointed in advance with the outcome of the Kennedy Round have raised for the first time since 1949 (when the United States committed itself to European integration) fundamental questions about the direction of American trade policy. If the Kennedy Round is likely to "fail," how should the United States respond to the new trading power of the EEC and to growing doubts about the Community's political orientation? If the Kennedy Round demonstrates that these new issues cannot be dealt with successfully by multilateral negotiations based on the MFN principle, are there better ways to further American interests along with those of Britain, Canada, Japan, and the European countries which are not members of the Community?

We shall examine these questions presently. Before doing so, however, a closer look at the economic interests of the advanced industrial nations in trade liberalization is necessary.

Industrial Trade Liberalization in the 1960s: Some Economic Considerations

Most of the advanced industrial nations are at a stage of development where, for a growing part of their industrial output, a high rate of growth depends on an expansion of output more rapid than is possible within domestic markets. Growing international specialization has become a condition of maintaining a high rate of industrial growth. This observation applies particularly to specialized industrial products, transport equipment, and highly differentiated consumer goods, and rather less to staple products of older industries, such as fabricated metals, textiles, basic chemicals, and standardized consumer goods. Specialized products account for a growing proportion of industrial output and play a "leading" role in economic growth. An explanation of this phenomenon would lead us far beyond the scope of this book. Yet its importance for the future of trade arrangements among industrial countries is so great that some discussion is necessary.

Tariffs permitting, a country imports manufactured goods which can be made more cheaply abroad and exports those it makes more cheaply than other countries. International cost differences result from differences in wage rates, in capital costs, and in raw material costs, and from differences in the productivity of labor and capital. Economies of scale are an important factor in the productivity of labor and capital. Other things being equal, the larger the volume in which an article is produced, and the longer the production run, the higher the productivity of labor and capital and the lower the cost of production—up to a certain volume, which may be very large if highly mechanized, capital-intensive methods of production are used. The availability of economies of scale, therefore, depends on the size of the market. The division of labor (which is the principal source of economies of scale) depends upon the extent of the market, as Adam Smith said two centuries ago.

Where staple manufactures are concerned, economies of scale are not so likely to depend on large export markets. By definition, the demand for staples is widespread. Nearly every industry uses steel products, basic chemicals, and textiles in one form or another, for example. All consumers buy clothing and house furnishings. Moreover, some staple products are manufactured by relatively simple, labor-intensive methods in which economies of scale are limited. Thus, except in the small industrial countries, firms producing staples can maintain a sufficient volume of production without depending heavily on exports. There is international trade and international specialization in staple products, of course, but it is usually the result of wage differences, or differences in the cost of materials, or differences in productivity owing to causes other than economies of scale.

The case of specialized equipment and consumer goods is different. Demand for such products is narrower. Jet aircraft, for example, are sold to a few airlines. Most automatic machine tools can only be used to make one kind of product. Highly mechanized, capital-intensive methods of production are the rule. Thus manufactures which can benefit from economies of scale are more likely to require large and growing export markets than do staples.[12]

These generalizations, based as they are on rather loosely defined industrial categories, are subject to many qualifications. They do, however, suggest an important reason why the advanced industrial countries are increasingly interested in liberalizing industrial trade, at least in specialized products. The health and vigor of "growth industries" depend increasingly on it.

Exporters of specialized products are less concerned with reducing tariffs than they are with assuring that tariffs will not be raised and that non-tariff barriers will not be imposed. Uncertainty about the future conditions of access to foreign markets rather than the height of existing tariffs seems to be the principal obstacle to the growth of international specialization in the critical industrial categories.

Tariffs on specialized manufactures have already been considerably reduced. A manufacturer's ability to exploit economies of scale can make so large a difference in his manu-

---

[12] One bit of evidence tending to support these conclusions is the extent to which international specialization in what we have called "specialized" products occurs *within* industrial categories. Economies of scale rather than other determinants of comparative cost seem to be the explanation.

facturing costs for products of this kind that a moderate tariff may make little difference. Moreover, non-price competition is more important than in the case of staple manufactures, which compete largely on the basis of price. Specialized producers' goods, such as modern aircraft, advanced machine tools, and electronic equipment, generally compete more on the basis of technological lead, reliability, or servicing than on price. Highly differentiated consumer products compete on the basis of marketing rather than on price. A large investment is often required to reach and exploit export markets for products of these kinds—in research and development, in plant and equipment, in overseas marketing, servicing and advertising, in complementary production facilities abroad. Such commitments require a feeling of assurance that the conditions of access to foreign markets will remain at least as favorable as when the investment was made.

The extraordinary growth of trade within the Common Market may be explained largely by the reduction of uncertainty. Trade in manufactures among the Six is increasing more rapidly than their external trade and more rapidly than production, indicating an increase in international specialization within the Community. These results have probably been owing more to the prospect of secure access to a greatly enlarged internal market than to the reduction of internal tariffs.

An arrangement which involves an irreversible commitment to free trade (or free trade in manufactures) among a restricted number of countries is the most effective method of liberalizing trade, not so much because it reduces and eventually eliminates tariffs as because it largely eliminates the members' uncertainty about the conditions of access to one anothers' markets. Eliminating uncertainty does not logically require participation in a customs union or free-trade area of restricted membership. In principle, any group of countries, large or small, could agree that any duty, once lowered, would never be raised again, and that no new non-tariff barriers would be imposed. In practice, however, what matters is the reliability and durability of the commitment. Escape clauses are frequently invoked, or non-tariff barriers imposed, when imports begin to hurt. A commitment within a restricted group is more reliable because the members' interests are more likely to be homogeneous. A commitment to free trade, although more difficult to make than a less far-reaching arrangement, is more durable because, once made, it builds for itself solid support from the broad spectrum of interests which it serves.

Only a restricted group of countries, already highly interdependent in trade, drawn together by a common interest in discriminating against powerful outside competitors and by a special political affinity, is capable of fully effective trade liberalization. The group need not, perhaps, be as restricted as the Six. Nor do the economic interests and political aims need to be as homogeneous as were those of the European Community at its inception. Effective liberalization based on a commitment to free trade would not be beyond the possibilities of all of Western Europe, if present political differences between France and Britain could be narrowed. It is probably not possible for any larger or more heterogeneous group—the Atlantic Community as a whole, for example.

The preceding discussion has special relevance for Britain. Of the industrial countries, Britain alone now has economic difficulties whose nature is such that trade arrangements might be critical for the nation's economic health. This is not true of any other industrial country. The United States, with its large domestic market, has no urgent general economic need for industrial trade liberalization. The same is true of the Common Market countries as long as the Community holds together. The small industrial countries, Switzerland, Scandinavia, and Austria, precisely because they are small, are often able to concentrate exports in a few products for a few markets where problems of access are manageable, although they, too, have a strong interest in trade liberalization. The British economy, however, is too large to follow the Swiss or Scandinavian example and too dependent on foreign trade to rely on internal growth.

Because British industry depends heavily on exports, the rate of growth of exports is critical for general economic growth. If the growth of exports could be accelerated and the higher rate sustained long enough to bring about a change in the expectations of British management concerning the prospective long-run growth rate, the vicious circle of low investment, weak competitive position (because of rising unit costs and slow technical progress), recurrent balance-of-payments trouble, and slow growth, might be broken. It might be replaced by a "virtuous circle," in which a higher rate of growth, a higher rate of investment, an improved competitive position (owing to a smaller rise in unit costs and more rapid technical progress), and confident expectations for long-run future growth would all reinforce one another.[18]

In Britain's present situation the only way a sustained increase in the rate of growth of exports could be achieved is by trade arrangements giving British exports secure access to the markets of the European Community. The prospect of secure and progressively freer access to this large and dynamic market might in time cause the change in long-run business expectations which is essential for Britain's economic health. The result could be an acceleration of general growth based, not on domestic demand, which would weaken the balance of payments, but on exports, which would strengthen it. So, too, increased competition from continental industry in British markets would help (as it has within the Community) to bring about the changes in spirit and attitudes which British man-

---

[18] This discussion is based on a model of British economic growth which Wilfred Beckerman explains in *The British Economy in 1975* (London: Cambridge University Press, for the National Institute of Economic and Social Research, 1965), Ch. II.

agement needs if it is to improve its competitive position abroad.

One cannot be sure that these results would follow, but no better alternative is in sight. Devaluation of the pound would probably not be sufficient. On the one hand, a devaluation large enough to give British exports a competitive advantage that would last long enough to bring about a change in long-run expectations would probably be too large to be accepted by Britain's competitors. Its effect on British exports would be partially nullified by the devaluation of other European currencies. On the other hand, a devaluation small enough to be acceptable to Britain's competitors would have effects too small or too short-lived to start the "virtuous circle" turning. Domestic monetary discipline and wage restraint are necessary but also insufficient, in the absence of a sustained improvement in export performance.

The American market would not be a sufficient substitute or one likely to be as attractive to Britain, even if the United States were willing to enter into a free-trade arrangement with Britain. British industrialists generally favor free trade with the Continent; they would probably support entry into the Community today as most of them did in 1962 were that option open. But there is relatively little support in Britain for free trade with the United States. Fear of the competitive power of American industry is not so great in Britain as on the Continent, but it is widespread nonetheless. What Britain's economic interests call for is membership in, or a preferential arrangement with, the European Community which would give British industry secure access to continental markets, plus the advantage of preferences against American and Japanese exports. If Britain joined the Community, or if the price of a preferential trade arrangement with the EEC was participation in the Community's Common Agricultural Policy, British consumers would have to pay more for food than they do now, when so much of their food comes in duty-free from low-cost American and Commonwealth sources. But the health of British industry is a more weighty consideration than the price of food.

With these considerations in mind, let us now return to the questions about the future course of American trade policy raised earlier.

American Trade Policy after the Kennedy Round

The prospective outcome of the Kennedy Round has evoked from unofficial sources in the United States several proposals for a drastic shift in the direction of American trade policy. The aim of these proposals is more political than economic: to restrict the European Community's freedom of action in trade policy or to counterbalance its trading power.

One proposal is to establish an Atlantic free-trade area for manufactured products. Its purpose would be to reduce the power and separateness of the EEC as a trading bloc by wiping out the customs union for industrial goods. Another proposal would link the United States, Canada, Britain, and other EFTA [13] countries in an industrial free-trade area, an EFTA on an Atlantic scale. Like EFTA, its aim would be defensive: to answer the Common Market's discrimination with counter-discrimination; to create a unit large enough in trade terms and with enough unity of purpose to balance the Community's trading power. Still another proposal goes by the name of "conditional MFN." If the European Community is unwilling to cut its tariffs as deeply as the other industrial countries, the United States would enter into reciprocal arrangements for broader and deeper tariff cuts with other countries willing to offer equivalent concessions, with tariff cuts generalized to those countries only, contrary to the unconditional MFN principle of the GATT. Tariff cutting under this proposal would

[13] European Free Trade Association, of which Great Britain is the principal member.

be too selective and too limited in degree to qualify under the free-trade-area exemption. Thus the arrangement, unlike the other proposals, would violate the GATT.

The Atlantic free-trade proposal is a logical extension of the policy of the Trade Expansion Act. Like that Act, its motives are primarily political. To be sure, the strictly economic value to the United States would not be negligible. But for an economy so vigorous, so competitive abroad, and at the same time so little dependent on industrial exports, the economic gains are hardly urgent. They would weigh lightly in the congressional scale compared with the problem of adjusting domestic industries to the removal of all tariffs on manufactures imported from Western Europe and Canada.

Like proposals to demonetize gold and restore the dollar to its former status, the proposal for Atlantic free trade seems to involve an overassessment of American bargaining power, or a failure to appreciate the attachment of the Six to their newly won bargaining power, with its overtones of political independence. As long as the Treaty of Rome is operative and the Six retain the hope of economic union, how could they give up the customs union which is the very embodiment of that hope? How could they now exchange the Atlantic for the European idea with respect to the only matter in which the European idea is a functioning reality? An American proposal of this kind for Atlantic free trade would be seen on the Continent by Gaullists and anti-Gaullist "Europeans" alike as a *machine de guerre* directed against the Community. The notion of Atlantic free trade, like its monetary counterpart, is interesting for what it reveals about American reactions to the shifting balance of economic and political power within the Atlantic world, but it is not negotiable.

The proposal for an industrial free-trade area linking the United States and Canada with EFTA may be more realistic than Atlantic free trade. The notion of Atlantic free trade ignores the conflict of interests between the United States and the Community and the Community's power to resist. The other proposal is based on the common interest of the participants in getting the Community's tariff down. Like EFTA, but more effectively, the arrangement would threaten the EEC with trade diversion. It might thus create an incentive to the Community to cut its tariff in exchange for equivalent cuts by the new grouping.

The purpose, then, is plausible. But the question remains whether the means are adequate and whether the larger political implications are in the American interest. In general, the size of the Community's internal market makes it somewhat doubtful that adding the United States and Canada to EFTA would create sufficient bargaining power, or power of attraction, to accomplish what EFTA seems unable to do. The trade in manufactures of the Six with each other is half again as large as their trade in manufactures with EFTA, Canada, and the United States combined, and has been growing a good deal more rapidly. The discrimination which the new arrangement would create would be felt in the Community but it would not constitute a threat to continued rapid growth. No doubt if commercial interests alone were involved, the Community, led by its more "outward-looking" members, Germany and the Netherlands, might be inclined to yield to the pressure which the new arrangement would create. But given the political importance which the Six attach to their customs union, and the resistance of France on more strictly political grounds, it seems unlikely that the tactic would be effective.

A more weighty objection is that a free-trade area linking Britain and the United States would tend to harden the present division between Britain and the Six and to foreclose the possibility of the rapprochement which Britain's economic interests demand and which Britain's desire to play an effective political role in Europe requires. For Britain, that would seem too high a price to pay for an increase in tariff bargaining power, as long as any hope of "joining Europe" remains.

Britain may not yet be as European as "Europeans" would like, but her long-run interests propel her toward the Six, as long as this can be done without losing the good will and the nuclear protection of the United States. For the past ten years Britain has been moving closer to Europe. The movement was arrested by De Gaulle's veto in 1963, but the trend seems unlikely to be reversed unless the forces of separatism and anti-Americanism which are called Gaullism eventually win out on the Continent. For the trend expresses fundamental British interests whose effective expression has been too long delayed by nostalgia for a more autonomous and global role now beyond Britain's means.

In itself and apart from its implications for European relations, free trade with the United States is relatively unattractive to Britain, on both economic and political grounds. British industry fears the American competition and the expansion of American ownership which would be the result of free trade with the United States. Moreover, in a free-trade area with the United States, the British would feel politically subordinated. Although there is little opinion in Britain which desires a separation of Europe from America, there are few Britons who do not yearn for more equality.

Free trade with the United States would be interesting to Britain if, but only if, she were convinced that major continental powers (not France alone) were irrevocably committed to a separatist course in foreign and military policy. In that situation, free trade with the United States might be the logical economic counterpart of a political realignment which ranged Britain alongside the United States against a Gaullist coalition on the Continent. Fortunately, that possibility is quite hypothetical today.

These considerations are as relevant for the United States as for Britain. Because of America's political interest in Britain's economic health, because of America's interest in increasing Britain's political influence on the Continent, any policy which diminished the possibility of British entry into the Community, or of a close trade relation with the Six, would be most ill advised. The United States cannot restore its own former political weight in Europe, but it can hope to increase the strength and influence of its most reliable ally.

We have stressed throughout this study the problem of reconciling "European" and "Atlantic" tendencies—that is, the interest of the United States in a politically cohesive Atlantic group under American leadership, and the interest of Europeans in autonomy and status. The hope of doing so rests heavily with Britain. The British combine the European and Atlantic tendencies in the manner and degree most acceptable to the United States. A United States–United Kingdom free-trade arrangement would be consistent with these larger interests only if all hope of reconciling the European and Atlantic ideas had been destroyed by the triumph of separatism on the Continent. In that dark event, much else in America's world alignments would also have to change.

As for "conditional MFN," it should hold few attractions for Britain or the United States. However disarming the name, it means scrapping GATT's primary rule, unconditional MFN. Any two countries would be free to make whatever preferential trade arrangements they might wish, even an arrangement covering a single product, subject only to the probably unenforcible requirement that the arrangement be open to third countries willing to grant equivalent concessions to the participants.

In such a trading system the contest would be to the strongest; that is, to the nation or trading unit with the most bargaining power. The EEC, for example, would be free to draw its small continental neighbors into a network of preferential agreements which would divert much trade from Britain and the United States. That this is no idle speculation is shown by the extent to which it has occurred already in the case of the Community's association agreements with Turkey,

Greece, and certain African countries (which are technically but hardly substantially within the GATT's free-trade-area exemption).

In present circumstances, the MFN principle is Britain's and America's best protection against the unfettered use of the Common Market's bargaining power. Those Americans and Britons who find conditional MFN attractive seem to be moved more by impatience with the EEC than by a sober assessment of what would happen if the perennial tendency of powerful trading nations to seek preferred positions in foreign markets were released from the salutary bonds of MFN. The rule of MFN has been one of the great accomplishments of American policy. It was possible only because in the 1940s the United States had the power to insist on it. Were impatience with the EEC or with General de Gaulle to cause us to allow it to be undermined, it would not be easily restored.

If this means being satisfied with slow progress in trade liberalization, as it probably does for some years ahead, that is a reasonable price to pay for tolerable order in trade relations. It is better to maintain a tolerable status quo than to risk a major setback in the illusory hope of major gain.

CHAPTER FIVE

The European Idea:
Theme and Variation

For two decades now the idea of European unity has played a major role in the politics of the Atlantic Community. In its classical form, the European idea holds that a supranational union is necessary for Western Europe's external security, internal political stability, and economic health. It is not primarily concerned with unity as a means to European independence or status as a world power. In so far as it is concerned with external political relations, it sees union as a means to more effective cooperation with the United States.

More recently another way of conceiving the European idea has come to the fore, with General de Gaulle as its spokesman. It differs from the classical doctrine both in purpose and in means. Its purpose is to build a Western European grouping which would be independent of the United States—a third great power able to look out for its own interests and pursue its own ambitions on the world stage. Although it would be called a political union, it would be, so far as foreign policy and military affairs are concerned, a simple coalition under French leadership. In economic matters it would consist of the European Economic Community devoid of any promise of supranational authority.

In this chapter we address ourselves to the prospects of the European idea, with particular reference to the classical and Gaullist versions. As we shall see, each involves a critical inconsistency—or a fundamental ambivalence—which casts doubt on the likelihood of its realization. Yet both express sufficiently powerful European interests and hopes to make it probable that they will continue to influence the course of Atlantic politics in the years to come.

The Classical Doctrine

The classical "European" doctrine was a response to the experience of war, profound disillusionment with European nationalism, and the conditions of Western Europe in the early postwar years. It took shape at a time when Western continental Europe was weak, divided, demoralized, and seemingly at the mercy of Stalin's legions. Germany was occupied; France and Italy were threatened by Communist subversion and neo-Fascist reaction. The war had destroyed much more than buildings and lives. It had sapped social morale. Many European institutions including the national state itself were being deeply questioned. In 1951 two contemporary observers reported,

The common denominator of these [continental European] attitudes is a strong conviction—not always clearly articulated but felt nonetheless strongly—that the national political and economic structure of the Continent is simply not adequate to cope with the rigorous world environment of the mid-twentieth century. The events of the last forty years, and particularly the experience of fascism, occupation, and liberation, seen from the perspective of postwar crises, have gradually sapped the belief of continental Europeans in their national state system. The average continental European feels himself a member of an enfeebled nation, the nearly helpless prize in a world power struggle in which his government plays no effective part. He knows that his economic horizons, his freedom of movement and opportunity are constricted within narrow national boundaries. He believes that the major factors determining his economic well-being, his military security, and even his personal survival are beyond the capacity of his government to control or even to influence very much. Unlike the average American or Briton, he feels that his national state is no longer capable of adequately discharging the increasingly heavy responsibilities of political sovereignty. As a consequence, and no matter how much the traditions and culture of his society still mean to him, his belief in and loyalty to his government as a sovereign political entity, his willingness to sacrifice and, if necessary, to die for it have been very severely impaired.

In turn, the effects of this loss of faith in the national state system have reached deeply into European life. A strong sense of confidence in existing governments and a strong, central political loyalty are essential to give meaning and order and a feeling of security to the life of every citizen. Without it the citizen sinks into political cynicism and apathy or embraces antidemocratic and antinational ideologies. Without it the economic incentives and attitudes necessary for a healthy free economy—confidence in the currency and the incentive to invest, to save, to plan for the future, to accept today's sacrifices for tomorrow's security and well-being,—are gravely weakened. Without it, confidence in the government and in political leadership drastically declines, its effective government becomes impossible, social cohesion is reduced, and class conflict increased. Thus, there has developed on the Continent a well-nigh universal sense of the inadequacy and instability of the status quo, felt even by the many continental Europeans who are not yet fully conscious that the source of their demoralization lies in the fact that continental European society has outgrown its national political and economic framework and can regain its vigor only when it finds some new and wider political form.[1]

Not all the early proponents of European union would have subscribed to all of these conclusions. Yet in the early

[1] Theodore Geiger and H. van B. Cleveland, *Making Western Europe Defensible* (Washington: National Planning Association, 1951), pp. 43–44.

1950s there was a broad consensus on the Continent and in the United States that Western Europe would never recover its military security, its political stability, or its economic health unless it established a supranational economic and political union.

It was assumed on both sides of the Atlantic that neither Americans nor Europeans would be willing to have Europe's security depend on an American guarantee secured by the presence of large American forces. The effect of nuclear weapons on the Alliance was not foreseen. "Speaking to Senator Green's Subcommittee [in 1951], General Alfred Gruenther said: 'General Eisenhower's contention here is that Western Europe must be able to defend itself.' " [2] "All of us someday would like to see the withdrawal from the continent of as large a number of forces as possible, if not in their totality," said David K. E. Bruce, American Ambassador to France in 1954.[3] Union seemed the obvious prerequisite if Western Europe was, without impairing its economic recovery, to defend itself against a totalitarian nation of 200 million, able to field (according to the contemporary estimate) some 175 divisions. "With unity achieved," said General Eisenhower, "Europe could build adequate security and, at the same time, continue the march of human betterment that has characterized Western civilization. . . . In such unity is a secure future for these peoples." [4]

Political stability, too, seemed to depend on union. If America's stabilizing presence on the European political scene could not be counted on indefinitely, what was to protect Europe and the United States from the consequences of Europe's divisions and instabilities? The answer which appealed to Americans and Europeans alike was to replace Europe's polit-

[2] Max Beloff, *The United States and the Unity of Europe* (Washington: The Brookings Institution, 1963), p. 78.

[3] Same.

[4] Address to the English-Speaking Union, London, July 3, 1951, *The New York Times*, July 4, 1951.

ical structure, "the rickety fire hazard of the past," as Secretary of State Dulles once called it, with a democratic federal union. For it was believed that a supranational union would be more stable and democratic, and more fundamentally cooperative and peace loving in external relations, than some of its component nations had proven in the past. To be sure, it was not self-evident that a powerful combination of Germany, France, and Italy—two of them peoples with no solid recent democratic traditions and with histories of aggressive nationalism and the third with a history of periodic authoritarianism —would be more consistently democratic and peace loving than the old Europe had been. Yet Americans had faith in the potential effect of American political forms on Europe's political spirit. The belief was firmly held that union on the model of the United States would transform Europe's politics and exorcize the demons of nationalism. On the other side of the Atlantic the same conclusion was reached by different reasoning. A doctrine of which Jean Monnet was the author held that European union would be achieved by an institutional method—the "Community method"—which would "denationalize" European politics and foreign policy.

Further and more concretely, European union was felt to be the only way to deal with the German problem. It was to reconcile Germany and France and to restore Germans to an honorable, secure, and non-nationalistic role in the West, in which their energies would be channeled into constructive pursuits and their national freedom of action sufficiently restricted to make further adventures unlikely or even impossible. With the American military presence in Western Europe eventually to be withdrawn, European union seemed the only way of forestalling a possible revival of aggressive nationalism in Germany. This was the aim of the Schuman Plan, Jean Monnet's stroke of genius which made practical politics of the European idea and launched the process of European unification. As Robert Schuman said in his famous statement of May

9, 1950, the purpose of the plan was to "make it plain that any war between France and Germany becomes, not merely unthinkable, but materially impossible." [5] This was the aim, too, of the stillborn European Defense Community.

As for Europe's economic health, the dominant opinion on both sides of the Atlantic was that Europe's economy could not be restored to vigor and prosperity until its narrow national economies had been combined into "a single market within which goods, money, and people could freely move and within which all barriers to trade and payments had been permanently swept away." [6] It was also widely assumed that the creation of a "single market" presupposed a broad delegation of economic sovereignty to supranational organs—in effect, a supranational economic government. [7]

Although the beliefs and assumptions of the 1950s are still in the vocabulary of the European idea, they no longer motivate as they once did, for they have been in large part overtaken by events. Unity no longer seems essential for security, because Western Europe has today an option which it did not seem to have in the 1950s—to remain under the American nuclear umbrella. As we have seen, political union in some degree would be necessary if Europe were to decide to provide for its own security—that much of the earlier assessment is

[5] Quoted in William Diebold, Jr., *The Schuman Plan* (New York: Praeger, for the Council on Foreign Relations, 1959), p. 1.

[6] Address by Paul G. Hoffman, Economic Cooperation Administrator, to the Council of Ministers of the Organization of European Economic Cooperation (OEEC), October 31, 1949.

[7] In the words of a congressional report: "It may be argued that effective free trade among sovereign states can be established simply by agreements to refrain from interfering with it. Such agreements can accomplish much in helping marginally to reduce trade barriers. Equally certainly they cannot create for the individual international trader or investor such a feeling of security, such an absence of extraordinary risk, as he has in doing business within his own country, and they cannot make adequate adjustments for differences in standard of living. The freedom of trade necessary for a truly unified market can exist only if such agreements are effectively—and that means *politically*—enforcible." Conference Report on Economic Cooperation Act of 1950, 81st Congress, May 19, 1950, p. 19. (Italic in original.)

still generally accepted—but there is no compelling need *on security grounds* to do so. Such is the present assessment on both sides of the Atlantic.

Nor is the economic case for political union any longer compelling. Experience has shown that neither Europe's economic health nor the creation of a common market presupposes a European government, even one with economic functions only. It now appears that institutions such as those of the European Economic Community today, which involve little delegation of supranational legislative and executive power, would suffice to create a European common market. The Community is essentially an intergovernmental organization, although a unique one. But its uniqueness does not lie in the possession by the Commission of legislative or executive functions, delegated by the Treaty of Rome or by agreement of the Council of Ministers. It lies rather in the Commission's role of initiative and leadership, formally conferred by the treaty and made politically effective by the commitment of the six governments to create an economic union.

The majority voting provision of the treaty, which took effect on January 1, 1966, was expected by some to move the Community a giant step toward supranationalism. The outcome of the crisis over this provision, precipitated by De Gaulle in June 1965, would suggest that it will not do so. The settlement of this dispute in January 1966 made a little less likely the always unlikely eventuality that a member of the Community would be outvoted on any issue it saw as seriously affecting its vital interests. But the relevant lesson to be learned, it would seem, is that the Community will go on much as before despite the *de facto* loss of this potential element of supranationalism.

External security and economic success, and the social reform which they have made possible, have restored morale and political stability in Western Europe. Even in France and Italy, with their traditionally alienated industrial working classes, the edge of class conflict has been blunted. Although domestic political life is not without difficulty, the improvement in comparison with the 1940s and early 1950s (and the interwar years) is extraordinary. The mood of continental politics today is muted, pragmatic, non-ideological, almost Anglo-Saxon. There has been no revival of the prewar variety of nationalism with its chauvinist, aggressive spirit and its ideological character.

Of the classical reasons for European union, only the argument that union is necessary to solve the problem of Germany's international role still carries conviction. Yet even this reason has lost its urgency. In the early 1950s war memories were fresh and everything about the character and spirit of the new Germany was in doubt. Since then the stability, the prudence, and the antinationalist spirit of German democracy have done a good deal to reassure Germany's Western neighbors that the Federal Republic is not the Republic of Weimar.

We do not suggest that this welcome development is a purely autonomous German phenomenon. It has no doubt owed a great deal to Germany's acceptance by her neighbors in Western Europe as a member in good standing of the various Western "clubs," including the European Economic Community with its implicit promise of political union. But the critical changes in Germany's external environment favorable to the emergence of a democratic and nonnationalistic German state have not been European in origin. They have been the Soviet presence on the Elbe and Germany's dependence on American protection. It is Germany's military dependence on the United States which has made it possible for NATO to play its controlling function via the integration of German military forces under SHAPE. The emotional commitment of many Germans to the European idea as the fulfillment of their desire for a final reconciliation with the West remains. But it is NATO and the United States which in fact exercise with respect to Germany the political function which Jean Monnet and Robert Schuman saw as the central *raison d'être* of European unity.

In sum, the ends which European union was to serve according to the classical doctrine have been accomplished by other means, sufficiently so, at any rate, to remove the urgency and dampen the crusading spirit which once characterized the European movement. The classical doctrine was surely correct in its judgment that nationalism and the national state, as they had existed in Europe before 1945, had become a dangerous and unworkable anachronism. But what the doctrine did not and perhaps could not foresee was the extent to which postwar conditions and experience were altering nationalism and the nation-state in such a way as to make economic cooperation effective without the need for union. Nor could the classical "Europeans" have foreseen the extent to which Western Europeans would be able and willing to go on depending on the United States, as guarantor of their external security and internal stability.

If Western European union seems less important or urgent than it did, it is because too much of what really matters to Western Europeans depends on the relationships which are extra-European. It is not only the national states but the European idea which has become too narrow for Western Europe's needs.

Economic Integration and Political Union

The implications of these developments for the prospects of European political union have been obscured by the classical theory of European unification. This theory holds that union will be achieved by a quasi-automatic process in which economic integration "spills over" gradually from one economic sector to another, and finally into the fields of foreign policy and defense. The theory assumes that the agreement on objectives necessary to support the process emerges progressively as unification proceeds. The process and the institutions gradually create the political consensus on which they themselves stand. The essentials of this theory were part of the intellectual equipment of many of the European and American officials most directly concerned with European recovery from 1949 on.[8] A belief that the process of integrating an important economic sector such as the continental coal and steel industry would tend to build support for its extension to other economic sectors and finally lead to political union was present in the minds of Jean Monnet and his collaborators when they launched the Schuman Plan.

The experience of the European Economic Community, brief as it has been, amply demonstrates the truth—and the limits—of the spillover theory. For example, the creation of a customs union among the Six tends to make it necessary to hold the general fiscal and monetary policies of the six governments more or less in line with one another. Otherwise changes in relative price levels, or in the relative pressure of demand within the Six economies, will result in large balance-of-payments surpluses or deficits within the Community. The governments cannot cure these surpluses or deficits by reimposing trade barriers without going back on their commitment to create a common market. Given the commitment, integration of commodity trade thus has a natural tendency to bring the monetary and fiscal authorities of the Six to recognize and accept the need for coordinating general monetary and fiscal policies. This is now beginning to happen.

Another example is the far-reaching effect of the Community's decision to fix common support prices for principal agricultural products. The common support prices are intended to carry out a common agricultural policy—that is, to yield farmers in the Community a certain income and to bring

---

[8] See, for example, Max Beloff, cited, p. 41. The theory was first given systematic expression by Ernst B. Haas, who coined the term "spillover," in *The Uniting of Europe* (Stanford University Press, 1958), pp. 291–299.

about certain levels of agricultural production and trade. These results depend on maintaining the relation between agricultural prices and the prices of nonagricultural goods and services throughout the Community. If the members were free to change the exchange rates of their currencies in relation to one another, the price relations on which the common agricultural policy depends for its effectiveness could be upset. Agreement on a common agricultural policy therefore creates an additional incentive to keep the exchange values of the members' currencies fixed in relation to one another. But countries which have bound their exchange rates tightly together have created something close to a common currency. For this to be workable implies considerable coordination of fiscal and monetary policies.

In sum, spillover works within the Community because as particular barriers to trade are lowered or particular elements of economic policy are coordinated, public and private interests are altered in such a way as to support extending the integration to other economic sectors. Integration of one economic sector or function creates pressures to integrate other sectors or functions. Economic interest groups, public and private, are forced by integration to see their interests on a Community-wide basis and to think in European rather than purely national terms. But the spillover effect is significant primarily with respect to economic policies directly related to the creation of the customs union and common market to which the six governments are committed. It involves such things as tariffs, exchange rates, direct subsidies, and excise taxes affecting trade, general monetary and fiscal policies. Beyond these economic instrumentalities and functions, the causal logic of spillover has only indirect and contingent effects, even as to economic functions. It has, for example, no necessary tendency to produce coordination of the composition of governmental investments or of the composition of national budgets, as distinguished from their over-all size and general impact on the level of demand. For such coordination is not necessary to create a common market and is not contemplated by the Treaty of Rome.

A fortiori, it would seem that economic integration has no strong tendency to lead on to political union, if "political union" means integrating functions of government primarily related to defense and political foreign policy. Integration of military and political functions is not a means to a common market; it is not implied by the commitments of the Treaty of Rome. It demands an additional and much more far-reaching commitment which the governments have yet to make. We do not suggest that decisions about integrating agriculture and money are not themselves highly political. The point is that these decisions have already been taken, implicitly at least, in the Treaty of Rome. This is not true of foreign and military policy.

Classical "Europeans" nevertheless still argue that spill-over will operate from economic functions to foreign and military policy. The most specific form of the argument is that the achievement of a common market will involve, in time, the delegation of broad supranational powers to the Commission, which will lead to a demand for democratic control of the Commission, through the European Assembly or an equivalent parliamentary body. The result would be an "economic government" for the Community, which, it is thought, would then naturally extend its powers to foreign policy and defense.

One difficulty with this line of thought has already been suggested. It appears that a common market can be created and the necessary harmonization of economic policies achieved with relatively little delegation of supranational authority to the Commission. Moreover, even if the Commission were to acquire substantial supranational authority, there is no necessary reason to suppose that this would lead to a decision by the member governments to delegate extensive legislative powers to the European Assembly, in order to balance and control the power of the Commission. It is at least as likely that the governments would prefer to exercise that control themselves through the Council of Ministers.

To be sure, if in time a group of European governments makes the decision to create a political union, it will most likely be the same group which has shared the successful experience of creating the European Economic Community. In this retrospective and contingent sense, it may prove true that economic union has led to political union. Prospectively, however, there is nothing inevitable and automatic about the transition from economic to political union. To hold otherwise obscures the need for—and the difficulties of—the political decision.

Political Union: Difficulties and Prerequisites

To establish a European political union which integrates foreign and military policy is a great deal more difficult than to create an economic union, even one with substantial elements of supranational authority. It is clear, in general, why this is so. Foreign policy and defense touch national interests which are more vital and more difficult to compromise than the interests involved in economic policy.

When an economic union is established among advanced industrial countries, the economic benefits and burdens are shared more or less equitably by the members, large and small. This is not true of economic power—the power to determine economic policy—which in an economic union tends to gravitate to the larger or stronger members, as it has to France and Germany in the EEC. But this element of inequity is not necessarily a serious obstacle to union, because economic power is normally valued more as a means than as an end in itself. If the economic union promises to bring large and proportionate gains in productivity and welfare to all the members, the fact that the smaller members lose control of their economic policy to the larger members is not necessarily an insuperable obstacle to union.

But the case of political unification is rather different. A nation's power to control its own military forces and manage its own external relations is generally highly prized as an end in itself and not simply as a means to security. If the Six, for example, were to create a political union, foreign policy and strategy would tend to be made by France and Germany for all. This is not something which Belgium, the Netherlands, and Italy could contemplate with equanimity—the more so because they have the alternative of retaining their political and military sovereignty under the American nuclear umbrella. To join the union would mean, in effect, that they had exchanged the rather easygoing and remote American protectorate for the closer and politically more dubious authority of France and Germany, made effective through the common organs of decision. In the circumstances, a minority vote in the common decision would probably not appear to the lesser members to be sufficient compensation for the loss of their autonomy.

For the larger members of a potential European political union, the difficulties of unification are also great. Although they would gain in power at the expense of their lesser neighbors (since they would now wield the power of the whole), the power they would lose in union is also valuable, for it is not largely negative, as in the case of the lesser members, but also positive: the autonomous power to exert influence. Moreover, the more positive character of their sovereignty brings them into conflict with one another about how the new power of the whole is to be shared and whose version of foreign policy and strategy is to prevail. Analogous difficulties arise in economic unification, too. But again they are more easily resolved because economic power is more instrumental and less valued for its own sake than power over foreign policy and control of military forces.

These general considerations do not mean that political union in Western Europe is impossible. They do mean that the will to unify must be both concrete and compelling if the inherent political difficulties are to be overcome. The motives for union must be very strong and relatively unambivalent, and there must be a concrete consensus on ends and means—that is, on policy.

As to motives, we have seen that the classical reasons for European unity have lost much of their relevance and urgency, in the main because the Atlantic relationship has proved to be more relevant than the European idea to Europe's most serious military and political problems. Nevertheless, the vision of "Europe" is very much alive. Indeed, it is now so widely shared by the elites and general public of the Six that it is no longer a radical idea. This is true despite the declining power of the original motives, because the European idea has come to express the widespread malaise Western Europeans feel at their continued dependence on the United States. For a younger generation of officials, politicians, and intellectuals, the force of the European idea is the desire for independence and for an opportunity to assert a European identity on the world stage.

The classical "Europeans" still see the political unification of Europe as a process in which technical institutions without strong political motive—or animated by a constructive spirit of international cooperation—would gradually assume the main powers of the national states, leaving them their historic and cultural identity but no power to do real harm. When the question of what political purpose would motivate this process is raised, they stress the goal of equality with the United States, arguing that the motive power of the European idea is the desire to achieve sufficient power to build an equal partnership with the United States. To this way of thinking it is repugnant to assert that the necessary basis of European political union is a European nationalism whose content is autonomy, power, and status for Europe as ends in themselves.

Yet why should Europeans go through the difficult process of setting up institutions to make foreign and military policy collectively, sacrificing their national freedom of action, unless for some exceedingly important common political end which they could not otherwise achieve? It is difficult to believe that the aim of equal partnership with the United States has the power to move Europeans to a grand act of political construction. Europeans already enjoy the security and prosperity which are the fruits of good relations with the United States, without paying the price of union. If they are to unite, they will have to desire intensely political fruits which union alone can bring: real autonomy, power, and status.

Will the motive of independence and world power status grow sufficiently to make political unity possible? On the present evidence, we are inclined to give a negative answer. The classical motives of European unity have lost most of their force principally because there are too many European interests and fears which tend to maintain the European nations' present relationship with the United States. There are malaise and ambivalence about this relationship, but that is a long way from a powerful and unambiguous will to do what is necessary to change the relationship fundamentally.

By the same token, the Six are far from a consensus on concrete ends and means to union. A shared vision is not a common policy. General agreement that Europe should organize itself to play a world role more worthy of its traditions is not enough. A consensus on *what* role, *how* to organize, and *who* is to participate is required to make of the common vision a common policy. On these essential questions the governments of the Six are profoundly divided. They are divided on whether the external purpose of organizing "Europe" is to induce or force the United States to accept a more nearly equal partnership (to share nuclear control, for example); or whether the purpose is to create an autonomous, third-force

Europe which would be as much a rival as a partner of the United States. They are divided on the internal institutional structure of a political "Europe," whether it should be supranational or intergovernmental. They are divided on membership, particularly British membership.

For the next few years at least no consensus on these hard questions is likely. The nations of Western Europe are too comfortable, too uncertain of one another, too fearful of the risks, and doubtful of the advantages of moving out from under the American umbrella. For the lesser powers, military dependence is less dubious politically than the idea of an autonomous Europe, especially one without Britain. For Germany, security is still too large a problem to make a clear choice for "Europe" and against the Atlantic relationship possible. Genuine autonomy in unity remains for many, perhaps most citizens of the European Six an attractive vision. It is not yet an objective of policy.

De Gaulle's "Europe"

If the principal motive of the European idea today is the desire for autonomy and status, it is not surprising that the Gaullist idea of "Europe" has a considerable appeal to Europeans, despite the fact that De Gaulle is so adamantly opposed to the supranationalism which, to the classical Europeans, is the hallmark of the European idea.

American power and Europe's military dependence give Europeans the feeling that they do not control their own political destiny. For the smaller European countries, the feeling, however, unwelcome, is hardly new. For citizens of former great powers it is a source of serious and growing frustration. The Soviet presence in Eastern Europe is less immediately galling, except to Germans. Yet a desire to end the European partition and to see a reduction not only of American but also of Soviet influence in Europe is a growing political force in all of Western Europe today. The partition of Europe between hostile coalitions seems increasingly to Europeans on both sides of the Elbe to be "unnatural, unhistoric, and contrary to present trends favoring not only European economic and then political unification, but, most important of all, the rapidly spreading psychological sense of European unity." [9]

President de Gaulle's design for Europe has attracted Europeans because it expresses these feelings and hopes, which they feel less free than he to make explicit. Germans are still too concerned about security to follow De Gaulle wholeheartedly, even if the General's ambiguous Eastern policy were less worrisome to them than it is. The British, with their sense of historical affinity to the United States and their doubts of both France and Germany, are still less able to be Gaullists. Yet in both countries and elsewhere in Western Europe there is a great deal of more or less ambivalent admiration for this harsh, authoritarian, but strangely impressive David who so impudently challenges the American Goliath and who seems to promise not only the withdrawal from Europe of American power but of Soviet power as well.

For these reasons, Gaullism in so far as it is the expression of Europeans' desire to be masters of their own destiny, is likely to survive its author as a continuing political force in Europe. But the Gaullist design of a "European Europe" based on a Western European coalition under French leadership is essentially unrealistic, because France lacks too much of the material power and the prestige which such leadership would require. As Zbigniew Brzezinski has put it, De Gaulle has a vision and a goal but he lacks a policy. He lacks the means, material and psychological, to his ambitious ends. [10]

[9] Zbigniew Brzezinski, *Alternative to Partition* (New York: McGraw-Hill, for the Council on Foreign Relations, 1965), p. vii.

[10] "Yet basically De Gaulle's policies—even if not his ultimate image of the shape of things to come—were contradictory and self-defeating. Having a clear goal is not the same thing as having a policy—although only too often his critics (especially in the United States) had instead a policy but no goals. The gap between French ends and means, preventing France from using economic or

It is tempting to explain this internal contradiction in the Gaullist design as the result of De Gaulle's attempt to have his cake and eat it, too—to wield Europe's potential power without sacrificing France's autonomy. There may be some such element of unreasonable hope in the General's thought, but the explanation is hardly consistent with what we know of his political insight and realism. A more probable explanation is the French President's sense of Western Europe's temper—its ambivalence about the notion of an autonomous Europe, its fear of weakening the Atlantic tie, its internal tensions and suspicions, its lack of a "soul" (a European patriotism, a European sense of mission), and of "roots" (a source of legitimate political authority in the will of the Western European peoples to create a new political community of their own).

For De Gaulle, European independence is the end and European unity the means. Until a European majority comes to share his view, a supranational union would not serve the purpose of independence. On the contrary, it would have the opposite effect. It would submerge France in a European majority which accepts the American protectorate. General de Gaulle seems to believe that without a strong common will to independence, no effective European government could arise. This seems to be the meaning of his insistence on the question of legitimate political authority. For the basis of legitimate democratic sovereignty is a common will to belong to an autonomous state. Unless that will exists, the attempt to create the beginnings of a supranational government for foreign policy and defense is, to his mind, artificial institution-building. Unless Europeans have the will to exist as an independent state, only the traditional nation-states provide a legitimate source of political authority. Without that will, a "Europe of

military power to pressure allies or to purchase friends, dictated not only a policy of sudden maneuver (for example, the exclusion of Britain from the Common Market) but also a posture of obstinate insistence on its point of view. . . . Thus although De Gaulle had a vision, he still did not have a policy. . . ." Brzezinski, cited, pp. 112, 115.

states" is preferable to a Europe united enough to restrict national freedom of action but not enough to do without American protection. From the General's perspective, a supranational political-military community would submerge the only European government actively seeking autonomy and put nothing strong and effective in its place. The new grouping, far from realizing his vision of autonomy, would remain dependent on American power.

If the union of Western Europe—Germany, Italy, the Netherlands, Belgium, Luxembourg, France—is a capital aim in our action outside, we have no desire to be dissolved within it. Any system that would consist of handing over our sovereignty to august international assemblies would be incompatible with the rights and the duties of the French Republic. But also, such a system would undoubtedly find itself powerless to sweep along and lead the peoples and, to begin with, our own people, in the domains where their souls and their flesh are in question. This abdication of the European states, of France in particular, would inevitably lead to subjection from without. It is, moreover, in order to avoid such an inconsistency and, as its consequence, such a dependence that we are bent on seeing the union of Europe constituted by nations which can and really wish to belong to it.[11]

Whatever the reasons for De Gaulle's attempt to do too much with too little, the result is the same—failure. The failure of his German policy illustrates the point.

De Gaulle's design requires a Germany willingly accepting of French leadership. When De Gaulle came to power, the psychological basis for such a relationship existed and may still exist today. Germany is still quite passive in her foreign relations, because of her sense of military insecurity and fear of disturbing her neighbors. Moreover, most Germans regard with profound satisfaction the Franco-German reconciliation. Psychology, however, is not enough. For his design to succeed, De Gaulle must offer Germans tangible benefits in re-

[11] President de Gaulle, Press Conference, April 19, 1963.

turn for political dependence: in particular, military protection against Soviet power. He must also be able to reassure Germany's neighbors (Frenchmen included) of his ability to restrain a potential future nationalistic Germany. These things he plainly lacks the power to do. In consequence, he has felt it necessary to seek in Eastern Europe and the Soviet Union other means to increase his political leverage on Germany. In so doing he defeats his own objective by undermining German trust in France.

On the one hand, he toasts Chancellor Erhard with eloquent words about the "cathedral," "the construction of Western Europe," which France and Germany are building together, whose "indispensable foundation is the reconciliation of Germany and France," and which is to be followed by the building of "another cathedral, still larger and still more beautiful—I mean the union of all of Europe." [12] On the other hand, he courts Eastern Europe and begins an ambiguous flirtation with the Soviet Union as though to say to Germany, "I have other ways of controlling you if you should refuse my leadership."

Such a policy is the product and evidence of weakness. It is an attempt by a relatively weak power to accomplish by maneuver what the United States is able to do directly by offering Germany a mutually beneficial bargain, in which American protection is exchanged for German acceptance of American leadership. In the end De Gaulle's German policy must be self-defeating, not just for his design but for French influence in Europe. Either it will tend to strengthen German dependence on the United States, or it will drive Germans to look out for their own security and their Eastern interests by a more independent and active foreign policy of their own.

De Gaulle's design would substitute France for America

---

[12] Toast delivered by General de Gaulle at the dinner given in his honor by Chancellor Erhard at the Federal Chancellery in Bonn on June 11, 1965 (New York: French Embassy Information Service).

as Western Europe's leader. But America's capacity to lead Europe is the product of qualifications, material and political, which are not easy to match. In a coalition whose functional purpose is military security, effective leadership presupposes not only the military power to protect Europe but the prestige which past military success and reliability as an ally have created. In a coalition whose ideological purpose is to protect democratic institutions, leadership presupposes the prestige of success in this sphere as well. French democracy lacks prestige even in France; De Gaulle has never concealed his contempt for *"les partis"*—that is, for traditional French parliamentary democracy. The American image in Europe is no doubt tarnished by many unattractive features of American manners and mores, but in the essentials relevant to leadership of a defensive democratic coalition there is no substitute to be found on the other side of the Atlantic.

What De Gaulle did for French morale and unity was of inestimable value to the West as a whole. His ability to see through the foggy sentimentalities of some "European" and "Atlantic" thinking has no doubt been of help to the West in understanding its condition. But on balance, his contribution has been negative. When he quits the political scene, he will leave behind him no positive diplomatic accomplishment for France, for Europe, or for the West, but rather a legacy of distrust and division among Europeans and between them and the United States. The phenomenon of Charles de Gaulle is perhaps not much more than a tour de force, in which sheer will has been made for a time to look like power and statesmanship.

In sum, De Gaulle sees that the "Europeans'" program lacks realism, because the European nations are unready to transfer their highest political loyalty to "Europe." But his own program is no more realistic, because when the chips are down the Western European nations would still rather depend on the United States for their security and political continuity than on one another. "Do the Europeans," asks Raymond Aron, "have enough confidence in themselves and in the Germans to wish for rather than fear political change, to rely more on their own capacity for defense and less on American protection?" His answer is in the negative, at least for the time being. Western Europe "prefers provisionally security in impotence to the anxiety and perils of a refound autonomy." [13]

Britain and the European Idea

We have left to the end of this discussion the question of Britain and "Europe," not because it is of less importance than the questions so far considered, but because it epitomizes them. For the obstacles which have kept the British from membership in the European Economic Community and from participation in European political unification are the same obstacles which have kept the European idea from realization on the Continent, in either its classical or its Gaullist form.

Earlier, the failure of British attempts to join Europe was owing to Britain's unwillingness to accept the supranational perspectives of the classical European idea. Today that obstacle has been greatly attenuated, because the Six, led or forced by De Gaulle, have themselves put off the question of supranationalism, even in economic matters, to the indefinite future. More recently, what has blocked British participation in the European enterprise is the other aspect of the dilemma of European unification: that a real European union presupposes the rise of a European nationalism, whereas the European majority prefers to go on depending on the United States, so far at least as defense is concerned. For the British, this aspect of the matter is more difficult than for continental Europeans, because of Britain's closer relationship with the United States.

To be sure, from Britain's standpoint there is no need to resolve this issue in its military or strictly political aspects in

---

[13] *Paix et Guerre* (Paris: Calmann-Lévy, 1962), pp. 497, 498.

order to join the European Economic Community, but De Gaulle has felt otherwise. His view has been that an Atlantic-minded Britain is not a suitable partner in *any* European enterprise. Nor has he relished the thought of sharing the leadership of "his" Europe with London.

Looking ahead, the most pressing consideration for Britain is her need for secure access to continental markets. The best way to meet that need would be to join the Economic Community. Britain's desire to play once again a significant political role on the Continent also pushes Britain toward the Six. So much is clear enough. What is not clear is whether and at what price France would allow Britain to join the enterprise of "Europe."

As long as De Gaulle cherishes his vision of a continental coalition led by France, the way is barred. For with Britain in the Community, Paris would have to share leadership with London. Yet were a future government of France—or even De Gaulle himself—to become sufficiently concerned about Germany, French interests might be seen differently, as under the Fourth Republic when the French sought (in vain) British participation in the Schuman Plan and the European Defense Community. If this were to happen, Britain might be able to join the Community without paying the price of loosening her political and military ties with the United States.

More realistically, perhaps, De Gaulle or a future French government would ask of Britain a measure of nuclear collaboration as the ticket of entry to the Community and the "European" enterprise.[14] Even after De Gaulle, France will no doubt continue to cherish the vision of an autonomous Europe. A European nuclear force of some kind based on French and British contingents, with German participation on

[14] After De Gaulle's veto of British entry in January 1963 there was a good deal of speculation that De Gaulle might have accepted Britain as a member if the Macmillan government had been willing to offer nuclear collaboration of some kind. See, for example, Robert Kleiman, *Atlantic Crisis* (New York: Norton, 1964), Ch. 3.

a basis not involving a national nuclear force, would therefore be a logical direction for French policy to move, if and when a French government decides that it wants Britain in Europe to help balance and control Germany.[15]

A European nuclear force might consist simply of British and French national contingents, or it might include a jointly owned and fully integrated denationalized force. German participation could take the form of financial and technological contributions, and perhaps membership on a control board deciding by unanimity, but would not include a separate or separable national German contingent. An arrangement of this kind would serve to inhibit a potential German nuclear force, while tending to restore Britain's influence on the Continent. It would be politically consistent with Britain's desire to join the European Economic Community and play a part in the European unity movement. Some support for Franco-British nuclear collaboration already exists in Conservative circles, and two former Conservative Ministers of Defense, Peter Thorneycroft and Duncan Sandys, have been associated with ideas of this kind.

If nuclear collaboration with France were to be the price of British entry into "Europe," the American reaction would probably determine the outcome. Neither Britain nor Germany would be likely to move on the nuclear front over the vigorous opposition of the United States. Both countries feel too dependent militarily on and too close politically to the United States to risk serious American disapproval in a matter touching the nuclear guarantee.

From an American standpoint, a European nuclear force is not the preferred way of dealing with the nuclear problem of the Alliance. An integrated Atlantic nuclear force along the lines of the MLF or ANF proposals would be preferable, as

[15] De Gaulle and his ministers have dropped hints from time to time about a European nuclear force, for which the *force de frappe* would be, in some sense, a nucleus. See, e.g., Pierre Messmer, "Our Military Policy," *Revue de la Défense Nationale*, May 1963.

we saw in Chapter 2. But an integrated European nuclear force with British participation would be preferable, from an American standpoint, to a German or Franco-German force, if that were to become the choice. Thus, if a new Atlantic nuclear arrangement proves in the end to be impossible, a European arrangement of the sort just described might be acceptable to the United States. As long as the European force remained small, as it doubtless would for some years, it would not qualify seriously American control of strategy making in the Alliance, and of the main deterrent, despite the absence of a formal American veto over the use of the European force. Such an arrangement would involve Germany and serve to contain German nuclear interests within a multilateral frame, although less effectively than an MLF or ANF would have done because of the absence of direct American participation.

A small European nuclear force would, of course, contain the seed of a large and fully autonomous European nuclear deterrent. But the seed is not the fruit and trees do not grow to the sky. The immense difficulties which lie in the way of European political and military union would have to be surmounted to turn a small European force of this kind into the principal military establishment of a truly united Europe. If European nuclear collaboration proves to be the only way to get Britain into Europe and to do something effective about Germany's nuclear role, the United States could well afford to take the risk that such collaboration might one day lead to the military and political separation of Europe and America.

CHAPTER SIX

The Atlantic Idea

Two conceptions of the Atlantic Community—two versions of the Atlantic idea—have prevailed in the postwar years. One is that the Atlantic nations are an incipient political community —that is, a group of countries taking the first steps toward political union. "The idea of Atlantic Union is on the march," said *The New York Times* on January 11, 1962. "Years of work and study will be required before the goal is reached; but the goal is no longer Utopian and begins to look like a historic inevitability." The second is that the Atlantic relationship should and will take the form of an equal partnership between a "strong and united Europe" and the United States. This view, unlike the first, has been official American doctrine since President Kennedy's speech of July 4, 1962, and less authoritatively for much longer. Yet a third way of understanding the Atlantic idea has been implicit in the preceding discussions of military, monetary, and trade questions. It is now time to make that view explicit.

The Atlantic Security Community

The nations which make up the Atlantic Community have long been conscious of belonging to a common civilization. Most of them, too, have felt a still closer and more exclusive affinity by reason of their commitment to democratic values and institutions. But until recent times their historical and moral affinities have had no great significance for their international relations. Before 1914 France and Britain were democracies and Germany, Austria, and Russia autocracies, but this difference did not determine their political and military alignments. National interests of a non-ideological kind—security, territory, prestige, power—were the objects of their cooperation or rivalry. Only transiently in World War I was a devotion to democracy invoked as a factor in international relations.

The change came in World War II when the Western democracies found themselves allied against a regime which sought not merely territorial aggrandizement or other national advantage, but rather the imposition on Europe of a totalitarian and imperialist new order. The idea of a Western community united not simply by a common military threat but by a common devotion to democratic freedoms was born of that struggle. It was perfected and strengthened when the Nazi threat was replaced by that of Communist Russia, whose thrust was even more explicitly directed at the foundations of Western political and economic order. It is no doubt the strong sense of solidarity created by a threat so systemic, so far-reaching, and so long continued which has given rise to the feeling that the Western democracies are destined to perfect their military and economic cooperation in political union.

Yet political communities are constructed of materials rarer and more durable than common values and common fears. The defining characteristic of a political community is that its constituents are moved by a loyalty to the community and the symbols of its unity and purpose (crown or constitution) as ends in themselves—not, to be sure, as ends above law and morality but nevertheless standing higher than any other political or economic interest or commitment. The Atlantic Community is not now and is not becoming a political community, because the highest political loyalty of the Atlantic peoples is to their national communities.

The Atlantic Community, then, is essentially a security community. Its political cohesion is greater than that of traditional alliances such as the temporary alignments by which the balance of power was maintained in nineteenth-century Europe, because of the long duration of the Atlantic Alliance and the ideological dimension of the Soviet threat. Its cohesion depends nevertheless on the sense of a need to stick together for reasons of military security. As the military tension and ideological passion of the cold war have abated, the political cohesion of the Atlantic Community has therefore diminished. The resulting outbreak of political conflict in the Alliance, although of a quite different order than the bitter national and ideological rivalries prewar Europe knew, demonstrates clearly enough the defensive and reactive nature of the Atlantic idea.

One implication of this view is that if a group of Western European countries were to acquire a nuclear deterrent sufficient to neutralize Soviet nuclear power, the political cohesion of the West would be greatly diminished, because the functional need for it would have been greatly reduced. Or to put it another way, the political cohesion of the Atlantic Community depends on the fact that the United States disposes of most of the nuclear forces of the Alliance. For Western Europe's lack of sufficient nuclear forces and its consequent dependence on American nuclear power are what create the common security interest on which political cohesion depends.

To be sure this would not be true if there were an Atlantic political consensus sufficiently broad and deep to make the United States willing to entrust the principal instruments of its security irrevocably to joint Atlantic control. But such a political consensus would amount to the willingness to create an integral Atlantic political community. As it is, the United States lacks the incentive to share control of its military power and political destiny, while the European allies have no choice (unless they unify) but to depend on American protection. The conclusion that America's nuclear preponderance is critical to Atlantic cohesion may be unwelcome, but it follows inevitably from the fact that the Atlantic Community is a coalition and not a political community.

The conclusion holds, notwithstanding the fact that nuclear inequality is itself a divisive force. The problem of reconciling the inequality which is necessary for internal order and external security with the demand for equality is perennial in any kind of human cooperation. In an integral political community, the problem can be solved by constitutional means which centralize control of military power in the legitimate authorities of the community. In a coalition, this solution is unavailable. The power of the United States in the Alliance cannot be based on legitimate authority; it is power *de facto,* not authority *de jure.* It is therefore highly problematic for Europeans and, for that reason, may be unstable in the long run. But the need for leadership, for central power, in any complex system of human cooperation exists whether or not the power can be legitimized. The Atlantic Community cannot dispense with the American nuclear protectorate, however irksome for Europeans it may be, without dividing itself.

A second implication of this view of the Atlantic Community is that its function is limited geographically to the area of the Soviet threat to Western Europe. For that threat is the Community's *raison d'être.* Other security problems impinge on the interests of some of the Western countries, but not as "Atlantic" or "NATO" problems. The Korean War was the last time a substantial number of the Atlantic allies felt a common need to act together to meet a military problem outside the treaty area. This is why so little has come of the periodic proposals to broaden the jurisdiction of NATO to include Western security problems in the Third World.

The notion of the Atlantic Alliance as the guardian of

Western security interests and the promoter of Western ideals around the globe is an attractive vision to which even General de Gaulle has not been immune. It seems to have been a part of his earlier, less "Gaullist" picture of the future, at the time he proposed that NATO's writ should run to the entire non-Communist world and that the Alliance should be headed by an American-British-French directorate.[1] But whether in the form proposed by De Gaulle or in another form, the idea in present circumstances is illusory. An Atlantic directorate could not function in the manner which this proposal assumed in the absence of an Atlantic consensus on major political objectives in the Third World, and an agreement on how to share burdens and benefits. No such consensus and agreement exist —note Vietnam and Communist China. In present circumstances a directorate would be no more than a forum for political consultation among the major allies. It would seem that they hardly need another regular means of talking to one another in Paris about political questions. The NATO Council and its committee structure already serve that purpose tolerably well.

By the same token, the American criticism of its European allies for their failure to assume a larger share of the responsibilities of the West in the Third World, although understandable, is somewhat unrealistic. There is irony, too, in this charge of irresponsibility from a great nation so recently emerged from isolationism, which actively encouraged the European powers to relinquish their colonial responsibilities.[2] But whether or not the charge comes with good grace from the United States, it is clear that continental Europe does not feel

[1] The unresponsiveness of the Eisenhower and Kennedy administrations to this proposal has sometimes been thought to have been a factor in De Gaulle's decision to turn his back on the Alliance and espouse his present line. See, for example, Robert Kleiman, *Atlantic Crisis* (New York: Norton, 1964), pp. 138, 139.

[2] As Henry A. Kissinger has pointed out in *The Troubled Partnership: A Reappraisal of the Atlantic Alliance* (New York: McGraw-Hill, for the Council on Foreign Relations, 1965), p. 8.

its own interests would be served. Europeans are glad enough to hide behind American military might, with freedom to criticize policies Americans feel are in the common good, just as Americans once deplored British colonialism while depending for their security on the royal navy. Nevertheless, the vision of mobilizing the whole power and prestige of the West under American leadership, to contain Communist China and cope with the growing disorder of the Third World, lives on in American hearts. A recent excellent survey of the problems of the Alliance could still maintain in 1965 as its "central thesis" the belief or hope "that the Atlantic Alliance is in transition from a regional security mission to the task of providing leadership in building a viable world order." [3] Would that it were.

The Atlantic Economic Community

The Atlantic Community is an economic community as well as a security community. The Atlantic nations have achieved among themselves a degree of international economic integration and cooperation which is unique, both historically and in the contemporary world. Western economic authorities have approached international monetary and trade problems with a presumption in favor of integrative rather than protectionist or autonomist solutions, and with an unprecedented capacity for cooperation. In the interwar years and particularly in the 1930s, the opposite presumption prevailed, and attempts at economic cooperation, such as the ill-starred London Economic Conference of 1933, were largely abortive.

As we have seen, Atlantic economic integration was initially facilitated and given considerable momentum by the dominant economic position and policies of the United States. Financial integration was made possible by the dominance of

---

[3] Timothy W. Stanley, *NATO in Transition* (New York: Praeger, for the Council on Foreign Relations, 1965), p. 395.

the dollar and the fact that the American capital and money markets were open to all. Trade liberalization was possible because the then-dominant trading nation took the lead. But apart from the initial impetus given by American leadership, what is it about the postwar world which makes Atlantic economic cooperation possible?

A good part of the explanation lies in causes which are economic or institutional as distinguished from political. We have considered the growing interest of advanced economies in industrial trade, which creates strong support on economic grounds not only for tariff cutting but for regional free trade, and for international monetary arrangements which keep exchange rates stable. Of still greater importance have been changes in national economic regimes and policies.

There has been a marked convergence of national economic regimes and policies toward a norm which, though it may be called "socialism" in Western Europe and "capitalism" in America, is in fact a mixed system whose spirit is pragmatic and unideological. The relevant features of this system are a commitment to high employment and rapid growth with minimal inflation; control of the general conjuncture by fiscal and monetary policy; private ownership and control of business, apart from public utilities and, in Europe, some nationalized industries which on the whole behave much as privately owned companies do; detailed market control by public authorities in agriculture but stress on competition as the principal regulator in the rest of the economy.[4] The diversity of economic regimes and policies which characterized the industrial countries in the interwar years, ranging from the *laissez-faire* capitalism of America in the 1920s to the New Deal, to

---

[4] There are other examples of convergence toward a norm in Atlantic economic policies and institutions; for example, the use of progressive taxation and subsidies to redistribute income in favor of disadvantaged groups; and large public investments in social capital and for the benefit of depressed or backward sectors. Those mentioned in the text seem to be the most relevant to international integration.

the corporative state of the Nazis and Fascists, to the stagnant and cartelized capitalism of prewar France and Britain, has disappeared.

This Euro-American economic system is hospitable to international integration. National economic objectives and policies are on the whole much more consistent than formerly with the maintenance of currency convertibility and with liberalization of trade, at least in industrial products. In these as in other respects, the Western industrial economies differ radically from the economic regimes prevailing in the rest of the world. Integration for the Socialist economies would require a common will to subordinate national economic plans to a detailed supranational plan—a will which they conspicuously lack.[5] Most Asian, African, and Latin American countries are still too little involved in a money economy, or are too short of foreign exchange, or have industrial costs too high to be able to participate more than marginally in the international economy.

In discussing monetary and trade policy in earlier chapters, we stressed the conflicts of interest among the Atlantic nations. Stress on differences is unavoidable when policy questions are being considered. But as we have seen, the differences take the form they do precisely because the Atlantic economies are relatively integrated. Indeed, economic integration in at least the present degree seems to be taken for granted even by the least cooperative of the allies. De Gaulle's France seeks to increase her influence over the creation of international reserves, and is determined that the European Economic Community shall not acquire supranational powers, but the French government has apparently no desire to reduce substantially the integration of Atlantic and European

[5] See Zbigniew Brzezinski, *Alternative to Partition* (New York: McGraw-Hill, for the Council on Foreign Relations, 1965), pp. 13–21. Hospitality to international integration is one of the great material and political advantages which the Atlantic nations have over the Soviet Union and its Eastern European allies.

trade and finance, from which the French economy has so greatly benefited.

Yet these economic and institutional factors do not wholly explain the Atlantic economic community. The political cohesion of the West is also a part of the explanation. It is clear why this must be so. We have seen that the economic integration which the Atlantic nations have achieved presupposes a high degree of economic cooperation. National economic authorities do not make economic policy in a political vacuum. If they are free to cooperate with each other, with primary consideration to economic interests, and to what we have called functional-political considerations, it is because the political atmosphere is conducive to it.

To be sure France's differences with her partners in the European Community over strictly political questions have slowed progress in European economic integration within the Community. So, too, the prospects of international monetary reform would be more promising if Franco-American differences over the objectives and control of reserve creation were not sharpened by a more fundamental clash of political objectives. But what this experience shows is that the Western nations' unprecedented ability to cooperate in economic matters is neither natural nor inevitable. Rather it has been an extraordinary political achievement.

The achievement has depended in the last analysis on the fact that the allies depend on one another for their security. In this sense the Atlantic economic community depends on the security community. If the military dependence of Western Europe on the United States were to terminate or to be greatly reduced, Atlantic economic integration would probably also be adversely affected. This would be true, at any rate, if the reduction of military dependence were the consequence of European political union conceived by a will to create a third-force Europe and in a spirit of rivalry with the United States. For integration in the present degree depends on a kind of cooperation which would hardly continue in an atmosphere of distrust and political rivalry. We do not suggest that important economic intercourse is possible only among allies, but the unique achievements of Western economic cooperation would not have been possible if there had been no common security problem. Nor in all probability would they survive unimpaired the military separation of Western Europe, or part of it, from the United States.

Although the economic community depends on the security community, its power structure is very different. The United States retains control of the deterrent forces of the Alliance, and that condition or something close to it appears to be necessary for Atlantic political cohesion. Initially, economic power, too, was highly centralized in American hands. But American aid, Europe's recovery, and the European Community have worked a revolution in the distribution of economic power in Europe's favor. As we have seen, this redistribution has not been accomplished without friction. Nevertheless, on balance, it has probably been conducive to political harmony in the Alliance, except where economic power has been used as a weapon in a more strictly political contest, as when France uses the leverage of gold to diminish the dollar's prestige. The division of military power would threaten the Atlantic Community's political integrity, but in economics it is the other way around. The division or sharing of economic power, because it does not touch the Atlantic Community's *raison d'être,* and because it is obviously more equitable, strengthens political cohesion. A more even distribution of economic power and, in the case of monetary arrangements, some degree of sharing of control of reserve creation, is desirable and indeed essential to the maintenance of the present degree of Atlantic economic integration.

Equal Partnership?

If this is true, the idea that the Atlantic relationship should increasingly assume the shape of an equal partnership between the United States and a united Europe requires considerable qualification. In military relations, the idea may have a rhetorical and propaganda value, but in principle it seems unsound. If a "Europe" existed able to provide a sufficient deterrent force of its own, a military partnership would be superfluous. The two powers might find it convenient from time to time to form an alignment against the Soviet Union or Communist China, in the manner characteristic of the multipolar politics of the European powers in the last century. But a relationship of this kind would hardly be a partnership in the sense intended by President Kennedy's Grand Design, for it would probably lack most of the political cohesion of the present relation. Equality there might be, but hardly partnership.

Indeed, the probability is that the relationship between a united Western Europe and the United States would be a difficult one. As was suggested in the preceding chapter, if a real European political-military union were to be created, it would probably be created in a spirit of rivalry with the United States. For if more cooperation with the United States is what Europeans want, they can have it without surmounting the difficulties of political unification or assuming the risks of dispensing with the American guarantee. In short, the concept of equal partnership in the military sphere seems unrealistic, because partnership (close cooperation) would be unnecessary if Europe were equal and because equality is unnecessary if partnership is Western Europe's objective.

In economic relations, however, experience has borne out the equal-partnership doctrine. As Europe's economic strength has grown, the United States has become more willing to adopt economic policies conducive to integration. It was in part the trading power of the EEC that made the Trade Expansion Act possible. The financial strength of continental Europe and the growth of European reserves have helped to persuade the United States that more shared control of reserve creation is necessary and that it can no longer continue to play as dominant a role as formerly in the management of the international monetary system.

To be sure, an economically powerful Continent is bound to use its power to further its own interests, not those of the United States. The outcome will therefore be different, and probably less desirable from an American standpoint, than if the United States were still the dominant economic power. There will be no "Atlantic trade partnership" of the far-reaching kind envisaged in Washington in 1962. The EEC is unlikely to modify its Common Agricultural Policy for the benefit of American farmers and taxpayers. Monetary reform, if and when it comes about, will reflect restrictive continental views of monetary strategy as much as America's and Britain's more expansionary views. Yet partnership—that is, cooperation—in these matters is nevertheless a living reality, because both partners, and other interested Atlantic nations as well, consider it in their interest to preserve a relatively integrated Atlantic economy.

If, then, equal partnership can be real in economics but is dubious in military matters, what should be the attitude of the United States toward the European idea?

American support for the European idea during the past fifteen years, has been a sound policy. It has helped to bring about the single most hopeful accomplishment of the postwar period: the rebirth of German democracy and the reconciliation of Germany with her Western neighbors. It has helped to convince Europeans of the non-imperialist character of American objectives in Europe. By allowing America to share with Europe in restoring Europe's sense of identity and dignity, it has helped keep the United States relevant to Western Europe's aspirations. This common political purpose, so natural an extension of the common purpose of the European Recovery Program, helped to give the Atlantic relationship a positive content which resistance to the Soviet Union and to communism could not alone have done. American support for the

European idea has thus been politically effective, even while many of the specific arguments originally made for European political union and the American interest in it have become irrelevant. For it was the American willingness to identify American interests and policy with the aspirations of the "Europeans" that mattered for the quality of the Atlantic relationship.

In the past, then, the fact that American support of the European idea has been rationalized in terms of a somewhat unrealistic doctrine of equal partnership was of relatively little importance. Perhaps, indeed, the doctrine has been one of those useful half-truths which, because it seems to reconcile inconsistent objectives, serves to oil the gears of diplomacy as long as the practical consequences of inconsistency lie in the future.

Today, however, the rationalization is wearing thin. The questions of European nuclear autonomy and of the political purpose of European unification have been seriously raised. Neither Americans nor Europeans can go on ignoring the inconsistency of the European and Atlantic ideas as applied to military matters. The problem can no longer be concealed by general talk of partnership or by theories of European unification which make it seem inevitable that, contrary to common sense and historical experience, the solidarity of the Atlantic Community can be helped only by European union. The trouble might have been postponed if General de Gaulle had not done his best to sharpen the issue. But the issue itself was inherent.

What this means in practical terms is that the United States cannot rationally support a degree of political-military union for Europe which would lead to a political separation of Europe from America. It seems unwise, therefore, for the United States to be as closely identified as it has been with the supranationalist strand of the European idea and with the classical Europe doctrine. The American attitude on political

and military union ought now to be more reserved and pragmatic.

But this is not to say that the United States should oppose
European political-military union in some degree. Because the
lion fully grown would be an uncomfortable companion is not
a reason to fear the cub—the more so as the probability of the
cub's growing up rapidly is not great. More positively, the European idea still has a constructive role to play from the standpoint of both European and American interests. As we have
seen, a European collective nuclear arrangement of some kind
may in time prove to be the only (though not from an American standpoint the best) way of coping with the problems of
Germany's nuclear role and of Britain's entry into "Europe."
Much the same could be said of the moves toward "political
union" of the sort contemplated by the so-called Fouchet
Plans, particularly if Britain were included.

In general, the best kind of political and military "Europe" from an American standpoint would be the one which
De Gaulle fears and many "Europeans" want: a "Europe" including Britain which is insufficiently united to reach for nuclear autonomy but still unified enough to go some way
toward meeting the European desire for political identity and
independence, while at the same time restricting German and
French freedom of action considerably. But of course it would
be unwise for the United States to voice any such thought officially, particularly as the issue is not now actual; even this
degree of political unity is not in prospect for the near future.

As for economic union, we ought to continue our support
of it, and of British participation. A European economic
union would help tie Germany to the West. As long at least as
Europe is militarily dependent, European economic union
would probably have a positive effect on the cohesion of the
West, although the degree to which this is true depends a good
deal on what happens about international monetary reform
and trade policy.

The Atlantic Idea and American Expectations

It might seem to follow from our consideration of the present state and future prospects of the Atlantic relationship that Americans ought not be particularly unhappy about the state of the Atlantic Community. Despite growing dissension, the basic pattern of relationships established in the early postwar years still stands, and it is a pattern consistent with the interests of the United States. American political leadership, the stability of the Alliance and the nuclear stalemate, an unprecedented degree of economic cooperation, a democratic and reasonably satisfied Germany—all these accomplishments of the last two decades seem likely to persist, at least for as long as the policy maker dares look ahead.

In fact, however, many Americans are uneasy and somehow disillusioned about the Atlantic relationship. Like Europe's malaise America's uneasiness has roots deeper than particular conflicts of interest. Nor can it be wholly explained by the fact that the tide of American political and economic power in Europe has ebbed, for the increase in Europe's economic and political strength has been a consistent aim of United States' policy. What seems to trouble Americans is that they expected something better—much better. They expected an Atlantic relationship in which conflicts of national interest, far from growing, would gradually give way to increasing cooperation and, in Western Europe's case, to supranational union. They were not prepared to find themselves involved in the seemingly indefinite exercise of power which is no longer unambiguously desired by their European allies.

In the heroic age of the Atlantic Community there were clear and urgent common tasks for economic recovery and defense. No struggle for power and control between Europe and America marred the relationship; Europe needed America too urgently and in too many ways to afford much immediate concern for its power or status. The European idea served to channel such concern as there was into the constructive task of "building Europe." Americans, for their part, hardly felt their leadership as the exercise of power. They saw themselves not as rulers but as agents appointed to carry out common tasks, an agency which America had not sought but history had thrust upon it.

Moreover, the inequality of the Atlantic relationship was assumed to be temporary. Either the Atlantic Community would evolve into a real political community in which power would be exercised, not by the United States but by the Community's legitimate authorities, or Western Europe would be united in a federal union whose power would be sufficient to balance that of the United States in an equal Atlantic partnership. With these assumptions, Americans succeeded for some years in avoiding the fact unpalatable to Americans, that the cohesion of the Atlantic Community rests on America's near-monopoly of nuclear force, and that the political power which nuclear monopoly creates cannot be legitimized nor can it be counterbalanced without undoing the Atlantic Community.

Today these assumptions are hardly convincing. Americans, like Europeans, are coming to see that the Atlantic idea involves for the foreseeable future an inherent conflict of interests, a dilemma which cannot be resolved: Western Europe's desire for autonomous power and status cannot be reconciled with the common security interests of America and Europe. The frustration of Europe's political desires has been and probably remains, for the time being, an unavoidable condition of Europe's security and political stability.

Americans are not happy with this discovery. The idealism in our make-up revolts against so realistic a view of the Atlantic relationship. Our democratic ideology rejects the thought that the continuous exercise of power—power which cannot be legitimized by consent nor systematically checked and balanced by countervailing power—is, for all its inadequacy and moral ambiguity, the only source of order in relations among states.[6] Americans want something nobler, more dynamic, and above all more just—that is, more equal. They find it difficult to accept a kind of reality in which fundamental conflicts of interest are not on their way to resolution. That is no doubt why we have so consistently sought to obscure the aspects of power and conflict in the Atlantic relationship with Utopian notions of Atlantic union or equal partnership.

The moral embarrassment which Americans feel about the exercise of power and the assumption that somehow conflicts will always be resolved have not infrequently confused official thinking and rendered our policy making tentative and ineffective. In the matter of nuclear control, as we have seen, the United States lost an opportunity in 1964 to strengthen its ties with the Federal Republic and its hold on the nuclear forces of the Alliance because the administration waited for a clearer European consensus which was not forthcoming. The administration took the unreal position that since MLF or ANF were something we were willing to do in response to Europe's desire for nuclear sharing, it would be inappropriate to press the matter to a conclusion. Our hope for a broader and deeper consensus, our uneasiness about asserting our own vital interest in nuclear control, led us into self-deception and a failure of leadership. The American dilemma in Europe (as in Vietnam) is the difficulty of reconciling the need to exercise American power with traditional American values which hold that cooperation and consensus, not conflict, are the norm in international relations, and that power without consent is *ipso facto* evil.[7]

[6] As Reinhold Niebuhr has written, "Liberal democracy is vague on levels of community above that of the nation because its characteristic policies of assuring both order and justice by a check upon power and by an equilibrium of power do not apply except in a highly integrated parochial or national community. . . . There is, in short, no way of applying the liberal democratic standards to the expression of our power in world affairs." *The Structure of Nations and Empires* (New York: Scribner's, 1959), pp. 28, 29.

[7] As Walt W. Rostow once put it, "In general, when Americans could move in conformity both to patent national interest and to familiar ideological principles, the nation has been effective; for example, in European policy over the

These traditional American values may also help to explain another attitude or expectation which endangers the Atlantic Community: the hope which some Americans have that a substitute for the Atlantic Alliance can be found in a European security arrangement between the United States and the Soviet Union. The hope is that the two great powers will join all the states of Eastern and Western Europe in a multilateral military guarantee and nonaggression pact—a European collective security pact in the Wilsonian tradition.

Collective security in this sense is, of course, an old idea. It envisages an undertaking directed not against a particular state or coalition but against an abstract "aggressor" who is to be identified as and when he appears. This was the concept on which Wilson hoped to build the League of Nations. It informs the Charter of the United Nations: the great powers which had fought the Nazis together would continue in peacetime to act together to deter any aggressor who threatened the status quo. Nor is its application to the European security problem new. Proposals for a European security system based on this principle have been put forward from time to time ever since it began to appear that the Soviet Union would not attack in Europe. George Kennan's European security proposals in the 1950s had the flavor of collective security. European collective security proposals were also advanced in Germany in the 1950s, in the hope that they would pave the way to German reunification,[8] and in Labour circles in Britain. What is new is a growing interest in intellectual circles in the United

---

period 1947–52, embracing the Truman Doctrine, the Marshall Plan, and the early build-up of NATO. Thus also in the early stages of the Korean War there was a convergence of military interest and more abstract loyalty to collective security and the United Nations.

"Where our interests, as we saw them, clashed with our ideal views we had difficulty. We were inhibited from moving effectively against the Viet-Minh in 1953–54 by (among other factors) a reluctance to risk American lives in a cause tainted with colonialism. . . ." *The American Style: Essays in Value and Performance*, ed. Elting E. Morison (Harper, for M.I.T. Center for International Studies, 1958), p. 297.

[8] See, for example, Fritz Erler, "The Struggle for German Reunification," *Foreign Affairs*, April 1956, p. 385.

States, where the idea is often linked with proposals for European arms control and "disengagement" of Soviet and American forces.[9]

This concept appeals to Americans troubled by the moral dilemma of leadership, weary of dissension among the Atlantic allies, and of trying to run an alliance which is no longer unambiguously desired by Europeans. It appeals because it promises to make leadership and alliances unnecessary except in moments of crisis. A European collective security pact appeals, too, to those Americans who see the shape of the future as a grand system of cooperation between a reformed and conservative Soviet Union and the United States, to keep the peace in Europe and in the Third World, both powers rid at last of obstreperous allies and of the blackmail of underdeveloped nations. Something of this hope underlies the thinking of those Americans and Britons who see in the proposed antidissemination treaty a substitute for new Atlantic nuclear arrangements.

This picture of peace by cooperation of the great powers is not unattractive, but it is hardly much more convincing in this form than in the form of the UN Charter. Collective security is based on the assumption that the leading powers will be consistently more interested in peace than in advancing their own political, strategic, or ideological interests at one anothers' expense. If this were true, collective security would work. Or, more precisely, if the powers always put avoidance of war or the risk of war ahead of all other interests and ambitions, peace would prevail whether or not the situation were formalized in a collective security pact. A European collective security pact, in short, would be a reliable basis for European security only if it were unnecessary.

True, the common interest of the United States and the Soviet Union in avoiding nuclear war lends a little color to the

[9] See, for example, Ronald Steel, *The End of Alliance* (New York: Viking, 1964), Ch. 6; and Richard J. Barnett and Marcus G. Raskin, *After 20 Years* (New York: Random House, 1965), Ch. 6.

collective security idea. Its advocates now hope to build on this common interest a new structure of European security without rival alliances. The trouble is that this common interest in avoiding nuclear war can be made into a force for peace only by creating a situation in which any hostile military act creates, or seems to create, an unacceptable risk of escalation to nuclear war. This, as we have seen, is precisely the function of the Atlantic Alliance and its military dispositions, which the advocates of European collective security would dismantle. A collective security guarantee directed only against an unnamed "aggressor," and without the support of an American military presence, would not make peace in Europe more stable. Nor would it serve the cause of "world peace" or "reduction of tensions," which its advocates profess. On the contrary, it would weaken deterrence by weakening the seriousness of the guarantee and making the risk of nuclear escalation more doubtful. In this imperfect world, when powerful rivals confront one another, peace by balance of power is the only reliable peace.

In the longer run, the possibilities of cooperation with the Soviet Union may broaden, as Chinese power grows. But even then the rivalry of the great powers is not likely to disappear in Europe. For the shorter period with which this essay is concerned, that rivalry will, it seems, remain a determining condition of relations between Western Europe and the United States.

The danger of the revival of the collective security myth is not that the United States is likely to endorse it officially, but that it will mislead some Americans into words or acts which undermine Europe's—particularly Germany's—confidence in the American guarantee. That confidence is the indispensable cement of the Atlantic Community, and the Atlantic Community is the basis of peace between the great powers.

The Atlantic idea has served Europe and America well. If now the Atlantic relationship is marred by political discord, we should not be unduly discouraged. Conflict in some degree is the usual condition of relations among nations. The present state of the relationship should not be measured by the standard of a period when Europe needed America too badly to be concerned for its political status, nor by the expectations of the 1950s which experience has shown to be unrealistic. If Europe is frustrated, if Americans are weary of dissension and of the moral and practical difficulties of exercising power, these are not too high a price to pay for stable peace, for unprecedented economic success, and for the strengthening of democratic institutions.

The choice we face in our Atlantic policy is whether we, who alone have the power to assure the continuation of these benefits to Europeans and ourselves, will go on using our power to do so—or whether because we hoped that the task would be easier or morally less ambiguous we seek to lay down the load, trusting in the good will of other nations to look after vital interests which we have become too weary or too confused to look after ourselves.

Index

Index

PUBLICATIONS

FOREIGN AFFAIRS (quarterly), edited by Hamilton Fish Armstrong.

THE UNITED STATES IN WORLD AFFAIRS (annual). Volumes for 1931, 1932 and 1933, by Walter Lippmann and William O. Scroggs; for 1934–1935, 1936, 1937, 1938, 1939 and 1940, by Whitney H. Shepardson and William O. Scroggs; for 1945–1947, 1947–1948 and 1948–1949, by John C. Campbell; for 1949, 1950, 1951, 1952, 1953 and 1954, by Richard P. Stebbins; for 1955, by Hollis W. Barber; for 1956, 1957, 1958, 1959, 1960, 1961, 1962 and 1963, by Richard P. Stebbins; for 1964, by Jules Davids; for 1965, by Richard P. Stebbins.

DOCUMENTS ON AMERICAN FOREIGN RELATIONS (annual). Volume for 1952 edited by Clarence W. Baier and Richard P. Stebbins; for 1953 and 1954, edited by Peter V. Curl; for 1955, 1956, 1957, 1958 and 1959, edited by Paul E. Zinner; for 1960, 1961, 1962 and 1963, edited by Richard P. Stebbins; for 1964, by Jules Davids; for 1965, by Richard P. Stebbins.

POLITICAL HANDBOOK AND ATLAS OF THE WORLD (annual), edited by Walter H. Mallory.

THE CONSCIENCE OF THE RICH NATIONS: The Development Assistance Committee and the Common Aid Effort, by Seymour J. Rubin (1966),

ATLANTIC AGRICULTURAL UNITY: Is It Possible?, by John O. Coppock (1966).

TEST BAN AND DISARMAMENT: The Path of Negotiation, by Arthur H. Dean (1966).

COMMUNIST CHINA'S ECONOMIC GROWTH AND FOREIGN TRADE, by Alexander Eckstein (1966).

POLICIES TOWARD CHINA: Views from Six Continents, edited by A. M. Halpern (1966).

THE AMERICAN PEOPLE AND CHINA, by A. T. Steele (1966).

INTERNATIONAL POLITICAL COMMUNICATION, by W. Phillips Davison (1965).

MONETARY REFORM FOR THE WORLD ECONOMY, by Robert V. Roosa (1965).

AFRICAN BATTLELINE: American Policy Choices in Southern Africa, by Waldemar A. Nielsen (1965).

NATO IN TRANSITION: The Future of the Atlantic Alliance, by Timothy W. Stanley (1965).

ALTERNATIVE TO PARTITION: For a Broader Conception of America's Role in Europe, by Zbigniew Brzezinski (1965).

THE TROUBLED PARTNERSHIP: A Re-Appraisal of the Atlantic Alliance, by Henry A. Kissinger (1965).

REMNANTS OF EMPIRE: The United Nations and the End of Colonialism, by David W. Wainhouse (1965).

THE EUROPEAN COMMUNITY AND AMERICAN TRADE: A Study in Atlantic Economics and Policy, by Randall Hinshaw (1964).

THE FOURTH DIMENSION OF FOREIGN POLICY: Educational and Cultural Affairs, by Philip H. Coombs (1964).

AMERICAN AGENCIES INTERESTED IN INTERNATIONAL AFFAIRS (Fifth Edition), compiled by Donald Wasson (1964).

JAPAN AND THE UNITED STATES IN WORLD TRADE, by Warren S. Hunsberger (1964).

FOREIGN AFFAIRS BIBLIOGRAPHY, 1952–1962, by Henry L. Roberts (1964).

THE DOLLAR IN WORLD AFFAIRS: An Essay in International Financial Policy, by Henry G. Aubrey (1964).

ON DEALING WITH THE COMMUNIST WORLD, by George F. Kennan (1964).

FOREIGN AID AND FOREIGN POLICY, by Edward S. Mason (1964).

THE SCIENTIFIC REVOLUTION AND WORLD POLITICS, by Caryl P. Haskins (1964).

AFRICA: A Foreign Affairs Reader, edited by Philip W. Quigg (1964).

THE PHILIPPINES AND THE UNITED STATES: Problems of Partnership, by George E. Taylor (1964).

SOUTHEAST ASIA IN UNITED STATES POLICY, by Russell H. Fifield (1963).

UNESCO: ASSESSMENT AND PROMISE, by George N. Shuster (1963).

THE PEACEFUL ATOM IN FOREIGN POLICY, by Arnold Kramish (1963).

THE ARABS AND THE WORLD: Nasser's Arab Nationalist Policy, by Charles D. Cremeans (1963).

TOWARD AN ATLANTIC COMMUNITY, by Christian A. Herter (1963).

THE SOVIET UNION, 1922–1962: A Foreign Affairs Reader, edited by Philip E. Mosely (1963).

THE POLITICS OF FOREIGN AID: American Experience in Southeast Asia, by John D. Montgomery (1962).

SPEARHEADS OF DEMOCRACY: Labor in the Developing Countries, by George C. Lodge (1962).

LATIN AMERICA: Diplomacy and Reality, by Adolf A. Berle (1962).

THE ORGANIZATION OF AMERICAN STATES AND THE HEMISPHERE CRISIS, by John C. Dreier (1962).

THE UNITED NATIONS: Structure for Peace, by Ernest A. Gross (1962).

THE LONG POLAR WATCH: Canada and the Defense of North America, by Melvin Conant (1962).

ARMS AND POLITICS IN LATIN AMERICA (Revised Edition), by Edwin Lieuwen (1961).

THE FUTURE OF UNDERDEVELOPED COUNTRIES: Political Implications of Economic Development (Revised Edition), by Eugene Staley (1961).

SPAIN AND DEFENSE OF THE WEST: Ally and Liability, by Arthur P. Whitaker (1961).

SOCIAL CHANGE IN LATIN AMERICA TODAY: Its Implications for United States Policy, by Richard N. Adams, John P. Gillin, Allan R. Holmberg, Oscar Lewis, Richard W. Patch, and Charles W. Wagley (1961).

FOREIGN POLICY: THE NEXT PHASE: The 1960s (Revised Edition), by Thomas K. Finletter (1960).

DEFENSE OF THE MIDDLE EAST: Problems of American Policy (Revised Edition), by John C. Campbell (1960).

COMMUNIST CHINA AND ASIA: Challenge to American Policy, by A. Doak Barnett (1960).

FRANCE, TROUBLED ALLY: De Gaulle's Heritage and Prospects, by Edgar S. Furniss, Jr. (1960).

THE SCHUMAN PLAN: A Study in Economic Cooperation, 1950–1959, by William Diebold, Jr. (1959).

SOVIET ECONOMIC AID: The New Aid and Trade Policy in Underdeveloped Countries, by Joseph S. Berliner (1958).

RAW MATERIALS: A Study of American Policy, by Percy W. Bidwell (1958).

NATO AND THE FUTURE OF EUROPE, by Ben T. Moore (1958).

AFRICAN ECONOMIC DEVELOPMENT, by William Hance (1958).

INDIA AND AMERICA: A Study of Their Relations, by Phillips Talbot and S. L. Poplai (1958).

NUCLEAR WEAPONS AND FOREIGN POLICY, by Henry A. Kissinger (1957).

MOSCOW-PEKING AXIS: Strength and Strains, by Howard L. Boorman, Alexander Eckstein, Philip E. Mosley and Benjamin Schwartz (1957).

RUSSIA AND AMERICA: Dangers and Prospects, by Henry L. Roberts (1956).

ABOUT THE AUTHOR

Harold van B. Cleveland has served as Assistant Chief of the Division of Investment and Economic Development, Department of State; Deputy Director and Special Economic Advisor, European Program Division, Economic Cooperation Administration; International Economist and Assistant Director of Research, Committee for Economic Development; and Counsel, the John Hancock Mutual Life Insurance Company. He is now Director of Atlantic Policy Studies of the Council on Foreign Relations and Vice-President of the First National City Bank of New York.